Three Ancient Colonies

THE W. E. B. DU BOIS LECTURES

Three Ancient Colonies

CARIBBEAN THEMES AND VARIATIONS

Sidney W. Mintz

HARVARD UNIVERSITY PRESS

Cambridge, Massachusetts

London, England

First Harvard University Press paperback edition, 2012

Library of Congress Cataloging-in-Publication Data
Mintz, Sidney Wilfred, 1922–
    Three ancient colonies: Caribbean themes and variations / Sidney W. Mintz.
        p. cm.—(W.E.B. Du Bois lecture series)
    Includes bibliographical references and index.
    ISBN 978-0-674-05012-9 (cloth : alk. paper)
    ISBN 978-0-674-06621-2 (pbk.)
    1. Ethnology—Jamaica.   2. Ethnology—Haiti.   3. Ethnology—Puerto Rico.
4. Culture diffusion—Jamaica.   5. Culture diffusion—Haiti.   6. Culture
diffusion—Puerto Rico.   7. Jamaica—Colonization.   8. Haiti—Colonization.
9. Puerto Rico—Colonization.   I. Title.
    GN635.J2M57   2010
    305.8009729—dc22   2009036043

In memory of
Taso Zayas and Elí Villarronga,
Tom and Leah Belnavis,
Nana and Jis Adrien

Contents

Illustrations

Acknowledgments

This book grew out of three lectures honoring William Edward Burghardt Du Bois, which I was invited to deliver in the spring of 2003, at Harvard's Du Bois Institute. I thank the Institute and its director, Professor Henry Louis Gates, Jr., for this opportunity.

I am deeply indebted to many persons and institutions for their assistance with this book, from its first conception in 2003 until now.

Professors Isar Godreau, Francisco Scarano, Kevin Yelvington, Jerome Handler, David Eltis, Stephan Palmié, and many other colleagues sent me information at times when I'd have been hard pressed to obtain it on my own. The staff of the Eisenhower Library, Johns Hopkins University, has been as unfailingly kind and helpful as ever. Though I single out Penelope and Bob Rickert and Yuan Yuan Zeng on its staff to thank here, everyone at "MSEL" deserves my gratitude. Among student assistants in recent years, I especially thank Brian Buta and Jennifer Malkoun. Tonnya Norwood of NK Graphics and copy editor Martha Ramsey greatly improved the manuscript by their scrupulous care and helpful suggestions.

Professors David Geggus, Barry Higman, and Juan Giusti-Cordero took pains to help me by reading and criticizing particular sections of the book, and I profited accordingly. Juan Giusti will never know how much his arguments have helped me. The Press's anonymous reviewer was generous, helpful, and exacting. Professor Rebecca J. Scott helped me uniquely. She read the entire manuscript; she found omissions and errors, which she graciously pointed out to me; and she urged me on throughout.

My wife, Jackie, suspecting at some point that I would never finish this book by myself, read, edited, and criticized. And indeed it got finished. It was meant to be my present for her; it has turned out to be more her present to me. I cannot adequately thank her.

Anthropological field workers never forget the people they work with in the field. They can help us or not. But without them, there really is no fieldwork. By their personalities and their acts, by the ways we come to know them, some become so important as to be agents of our own self-respect, and contributors to our own identity. Among my friends of this kind were Taso Zayas and Elí Villarronga in Puerto Rico, Tom and Leah Belnavis in Jamaica, and Nana and Gustave Adrien in Haiti. I owe them so much. I shall never forget them.

Three Ancient Colonies

Caribbean Anthropology and History

WILLIAM EDWARD BURGHARDT DU BOIS was thirty-two years old at the dawn of the twentieth century, to which we bade farewell only recently. Soon after, he published *The Souls of Black Folk* (Du Bois 1903). He began with a brief foreword, in which he wrote how, if one read with patience, one would find "the strange meaning of being black here in the dawning of the Twentieth Century. This meaning is not without interest to you, Gentle reader; for the problem of the Twentieth Century is the problem of the color-line" (1903:v). It is early enough in the twenty-first for us to wonder whether this century will be genuinely different.[1]

Du Bois grasped the implications of an American hemisphere that extended thousands of miles beyond the United States, populated in large measure by peoples of color. In advance of most of his compatriots, he drank in the meaning of the immense scale of slavery: its demographic consequences, and how its brutal history would continue to impose a crushing weight upon the present. It was slavery—owning other human beings as property, like land, cattle, or tools—that led to the birth of the black Americas, during the lengthy hemispheric oppression of African Americans. Du Bois understood that the need for cheap, defenseless labor—the original and only real reason why enslaved Africans were dragged to the Americas—had set the initial terms for the geography of Afro-America. Du Bois also understood that the countries lying within Indo-America, Mestizo America, and Afro-America (Service 1955), many of them once slaveholding, stood in ongoing and evolving relationships to the United States. He knew, too, that a politically hegemonic policy for the Americas, beginning with the Monroe Doctrine set forth in 1823, was the lasting background for U.S.-Caribbean relationships. Were he alive now, he would see how that policy, dubious both legally and ethically, is managed to this day in Guantánamo, Puerto Rico, the American Virgin Islands, and elsewhere.[2]

The Caribbean islands and nearby parts of the mainland coast make up a geographically modest but historically important region within the vast terrain of Afro-America. It is a region with which Du Bois's personal history was much entangled. On his father's side he had close relatives linked to postrevolutionary Saint Domingue, that ancient and once hugely lucrative colony that in 1804 became the Republic of Haiti. Du Bois's grandfather, Alexander Du Bois, lived in Haiti for more than a decade, though we know little of his years there. David Lewis (1993), W. E. B. Du Bois's biographer, writes that Alexander went to Haiti to salvage what he could of the property of his own long-dead father and W. E. B. Du Bois's great-grandfather—a physician of French origin and resident of New York, who had remained loyal to Great Britain at the time of the American Revolution. Dr. James Du Bois's royalist sympathies had gotten him land and slaves in the Bahamas, and he acquired additional wealth in French Saint Domingue. But when Alexander went there to see if anything was left for him after the Haitian Revolution, apparently there was little or nothing he could claim.

During those years in Haiti, however, he fathered Alfred, W. E. B. Du Bois's father, doubtless by a Haitian mother.[3] Alexander was already married when he went to Haiti; he had left his American family in New Haven, and would eventually return there, without his Haitian relatives. W. E. B. Du Bois, keenly sensitive about this murky tableau, was evasive when he wrote about his family background. Lewis notes that his vague and changing references to the paternal side of his family were sometimes handled as fact, and other times as fancy, in what he wrote. What facts there are suggest that Alfred, Du Bois's father, had led a rather aimless life. He had come from Haiti to the United States—but it is not clear where or when he arrived, or where he met the woman who became Du Bois's mother. Alfred appears to have abandoned them both eventually, although Du Bois (1968:72–73) puts a different ending to that story.

Alexander, W. E. B. Du Bois's grandfather, whom he knew about only from hearsay until his teens, turned out to be a dour kinsman, who was then living a robustly upright life in New Bedford. On his first and only visit there, Du Bois laid claim in his mind to everything he saw and heard in the house of his grandfather. Lewis is convincing when he suggests that Alexander's stern demeanor and the careful behavior of his wife and his colored neighbors lent to his fatherless, adolescent grandson a sense of self-respect and of family, of which he was in desperate need at the time (Lewis 1993:40–43).

Du Bois himself would learn of the Caribbean region both by reading and by travel. In 1915 when he visited Jamaica, he was received by Lord (Sidney Haldane) Olivier, Jamaica's Fabian socialist governor at the time, and was able to meet Marcus Garvey. In Jamaica, he later told *Crisis* readers, for the first time in his life he had "lived beyond the color line" (Lewis 1993:456). That visit seems to have impressed him—too much, perhaps. It seems that he never forgot his feelings on finding himself for the first time in a country with a predominant nonwhite majority. Jamaica was an ancient colony. But it was also a black nation with an elite of its own: writers, businessmen, physicians, journalists, artists, barristers, political leaders. In spite of the colonial setting and the small but disproportionately powerful white community, the quality of daily life in Jamaica seems to have given to Du Bois a deep sense of personal hope and reassurance that he was fated never to feel in the United States.

Du Bois's links to the black Americas were many.[4] While writing his doctoral thesis at Harvard on the slave trade to the New World, he learned how far-flung and enduring had been the empire of the whip. Born in 1868, soon after the U.S. Civil War, he was nearly twenty years old by the time Cuba finally ended slavery in 1886; and he had just turned twenty when Brazilian abolition brought the institution to an end in the Western Hemisphere, two years later.

From other scholars, especially Columbia anthropologist Franz Boas, Du Bois learned of the civilizational importance of Africa.[5] Throughout his life, his fascination with Africa outweighed his interest in the Caribbean region. Nonetheless, Du Bois recognized the historical significance of the Antilles, which in the seventeenth and eighteenth centuries were an early seedbed of European capitalism, soil watered and nourished with the sweat and blood of slaves.

Du Bois also learned that the Haitian Revolution, once won, was an ideological touchstone for New World black resistance (Geggus 1997; Scott 1986).[6] In his remarkable book *Black Folk, Then and Now* (1939) he deals with the Caribbean and with African peoples and histories. Seventy years ago, that book was surely the first serious global overview of African (and especially African-American) history ever published. My esteem for Du Bois's vision informed the writing of this book.

The history of the Caribbean region, in which the three societies I discuss are found, embodies the real beginnings of European overseas imperial rule. With some important exceptions to which I will refer again (such as the Canary Islands or Madeira), the modern world's first colonies are to be found mainly in the Caribbean region. More so than Europeans, and simply because of where they live, North Americans are not entirely aware of this. We are more under the spell than we realize of our own somewhat mythical chronology. For example, the year 1619 stands out for us—when the first enslaved Africans were brought ashore at Jamestown. Yet by that same year, Spanish Santo Domingo had been a European colony for more than 120 years; the Hispanic Caribbean had been shipping the New World's first sugar, made by African slaves, to Spain for more than a century.

Not only did most of the islands become colonial early,[7] most of them also stayed colonial late. Barbados became British around 1627, but it did not get its independence until 1966. Puerto Rico became colonial in 1509, and has never been politically independent. The North American view of New World history often discounts the European presence, but that presence was of course very significant—as the languages of the New World as well as its diversified cultures make so evident. Spain preceded everyone else in the Americas, but would be followed in a century by her northern European rivals. The marks of European power and culture remain significant and visible in much of the hemisphere, including the islands. Indeed, much of what is now "our" America we took, or bought at bargain prices from, our European contemporaries. (Of course, they had earlier taken it from the Native American peoples who had settled it.) But politically, the rebellious Englishmen ended up becoming "Americans," not Europeans—as did the Hispanic colonists of the Caribbean (Cuba, Haiti, the Dominican Republic) and the mainland to our south. The North American idea that the word "American," used adjectivally, is theirs alone other Americans resent.

People in erstwhile colonial areas besides North America may be slow to grasp how anciently colonial the Caribbean region is. The Indian subcontinent is usually thought to have become a colonial possession, mostly of Great Britain, when Clive defeated the nawab of Bengal at the battle of Plassey in 1757. Yet by 1757 the Antilles had been colonial for more than 250 years. Africa provides a different kind of contrast. Most of West Africa had not been conquered by the Europeans until nearly the end of the nineteenth century and, as with much of India, few Europeans ever really settled there. Yet large parts of West Africa won political independence soon after World War II, while much of the Caribbean remained colonial. These varied colonial experiences thus provide useful contrasts for thinking about the Caribbean. Once it can be acknowledged that Caribbean colonialism is truly ancient, its history can help to give additional nuance to the term "postcolonial."

Installing a comparative time dimension within colonial histories matters, partly because in the story of each colony, where the colonizing empire stood when a new colony fell into (or out of) its hands was a real factor in the colony's future. What colonies were, and what they became, still needs to be pondered, for the cultural overlay created by colonialism has had a long, disguised, and still often unconsidered afterlife (Cooper 2005).

The societies of the Caribbean shared with other societies, such as Brazil, Mexico, and the United States, their being part of what soon came to be called the "New World." The discovery of the Americas by the Europeans was momentous. But of course the hemisphere was not discovered in its entirety at the same moment, or colonized in the same manner, or all harnessed to European uses in the same way. Thus the Caribbean region emerges as a first chapter—possibly a qualitatively different chapter—in the history of European colonialism (Zeuske 2006). I believe its earliest decisive moments, economically and socially, took shape more than a century before the American Revolution.

That the Columbian discovery of the New World should have compelled Europe radically to reorient itself to the entire globe is now a platitude. But Europe remained centered on itself, and European history has always been written from the vantage point of Europe. It followed that world history as interpreted in the West by Europeans would, to a remarkable extent, be written mostly from the same perspective. Between the end of the fifteenth century and sometime late in the twentieth, I do not think that there was any more intelligently comprehensive view of the globe available to us. Only recently have scholars been able to begin to think seriously about a world history not centered on any single region; about the world-historical role of extra-European regions; and about the significance of the early colonial areas for modern imperial systems, in the later history of those empires.[8]

It was near the end of the fifteenth century that Columbus reached the islands that would one day be called Caribbean. Circumnavigation of Africa and soon after of the entire Earth followed. Historian Richard Konetzke pointed out (1946) that before Columbus, there had been no planetary (transoceanic) empires, only those built around seas. The bodies of water of primary concern to Europe were the Mediterranean and North seas. But after 1492 the Mediterranean was redefined as a geopolitically different body of water, and its place in world political and economic life was somewhat diminished, at least until much later in history. The West's orientation had become oceanic.

Though of course parts of it had been traversed earlier, the Atlantic Ocean began to become more fully European after 1492. After the Pacific was added—and that was very soon after—the world's globality became demonstrated as well as known, and the two New World continents became a western flank against which Europe and Africa on the one hand, and Asia on the other, were then counterposed.

Between 1492—when Columbus left one of his ship's crews on the island of Española (Santo Domingo)—and 1898, when the North Americans invaded Spain's two remaining New World colonies, both of them Antillean and insular,[9] the Atlantic's western littoral was of consummate interest to Europe. Over time, however, European zeal lessened. By the first half of the nineteenth century, and especially after the Haitian Revolution, Europe's view of the Americas had come up against some uncomfortable realities. That revolution had brought increased vigilance throughout the slaveholding Americas (including the United States)—heightened awareness on the part of the slave owners and hope among the enslaved. And from the mid-nineteenth century on, white North Americans, some painfully aware of the reality of a sovereign Haiti, pondered the appealing idea of Cuba or Santo Domingo as a United States–owned slave plantation colony. Nothing came of these imaginings. The decline of national protectionism for sugar and growing North American imperial ambitions during this era kept pace with the successive elimination of European slave systems in the Caribbean—British, Danish, French, and Dutch and, after the U.S. Civil War, in the remaining Hispanic colonies. It was after that war that the United States began its serious efforts to remake the Caribbean Sea as a North American lake.

The seesaw fate of the region, its profitability for its European masters declining even while its geopolitical and economic value to the United States rose, reminds us of the advantages of hindsight. We might claim that Columbus was wrongheaded to have sailed so far south. Instead of ending up in what would become the United States, he merely stumbled upon a handful of tiny islands, obdurately misdefined them as part of Asia, and failed to predict the future glory of what would first become the thirteen revolutionary British northern colonies, then the regnant independent and slave-holding nation, and eventually the superpower everyone now knows well.

But we must excuse Columbus. Those tiny islands he did find were to become among the most profitable possessions the Europeans ever wrested from the non-Western world—especially striking in view of their modest size. They were made lucrative by virtue of their fertile soil, ample water and wood, benign climate, and other natural resources. But there had to be imposed on them the acquisitive energy of European masters and the cumulative forced labor of millions of workers, nearly all of them African, torn from their homes so they would work for nothing for the Europeans. And it was those islands and forced laborers who brought forth the first commercially marketed soft drugs, which the world soon came to know and love: tobacco, coffee, chocolate, and the sugar and molasses needed to sweeten them.[10] In the centuries when the northern colonies were still acquiring what would be their characteristic shape, the Caribbean islands became bountiful agricultural factories of precious commodities. And so by 1619, when the first North American–enslaved Africans reached Jamestown, Caribbean plantation products were already long familiar in Europe, providing much profit in the colonies and radically changing European food habits.

The open sesame of European rule and profit in the Caribbean region was based on three things: slavery, sugar, and the agroindustrial enterprise called the plantation. But because so many studies of the Caribbean have made these very things the centerpiece of their analyses, it is important to recognize that many islands and subregions there did not become part of the slavery-sugar-plantation complex. In presenting information on the three islands I deal with here, I will try to distinguish among their histories, for this and other reasons. The relative weakness or absence of the plantation system in certain periods is itself a useful analytic key. The three ancient societies that concern me here differed in the roles that slavery, sugar, and the plantation would play in their history. Such differences were deep, and they were more than economic in nature.

At the same time, there is no challenging the immense importance of slavery, sugar, and the plantation in Caribbean life, especially in certain periods. I have argued elsewhere that the Caribbean sugar plantation had the effect of modernizing the people forced to work on it, and much of that modernity originated in the ways that slavery worked (Mintz 1996; Scott 2004). By forcibly drawing together people from scores, possibly even hundreds, of different cultures and languages, compelling them not only to labor ceaselessly on the plantations but also to craft for themselves new ways of life under terrible circumstances, the planter class imposed special conditions for daily living—indeed for survival itself—upon the African captives. The work regimen made the slaves into anonymous units of labor—alienated, expendable, interchangeable—as if they lacked individuality or any personal past. In the ways that the sugar plantations operated, these alienated laborers acquired an "industrial" time consciousness. They were commonly undernourished, deprived of sleep and adequate food, often beaten—and learned to survive under those conditions.

I argue further that these people developed a distinctive individuality of a kind that, when combined with the conditions of their labor, would modernize them in a particular way, born out of the loss of many of their original sources of identity, such as kinship, locality, and specific social and cultural contexts—their feelings of belonging to some specific place, time, and social group—and the emerging need to "reinvent" themselves under those conditions. That is to say, their reborn and distinctive individuality arose partly in reaction to the nearly total loss of historical continuity. Because of such drastic changes in the life conditions of millions of enslaved people, I will argue that the Caribbean region represented a distinct chapter in New World and colonial history. Other scholars, particularly the great Trinidadian writer and historian C. L. R. James, have said some of this. In an appendix to his famed work *The Black Jacobins,* James writes:

> The sugar plantation has been the most civilising as well as the most demoralising influence in West Indian development. When three centuries ago the slaves came to the West Indies,

they entered directly into the large-scale agriculture of the sugar plantation, which was a modern system. It further required that the slaves live together in a social relation far closer than any proletariat of the time. The cane when reaped had to be rapidly transported to what was factory production. The product was shipped abroad for sale. Even the cloth the slaves wore and the food they ate was imported. The Negroes, therefore, from the very start lived a life that was in its essence a modern life. That is their history—as far as I have been able to discover, a unique history. (1963:392)[11]

Yet in contrast to this picture, and in those parts of the region lying outside the plantation complex—too mountainous, too poorly watered, or otherwise unsuited for the sugar industry—other human communities developed differently. I will want to make as visible as possible what those differences were, because they represent the ways that local people, even those not within the plantation system itself, could resist the plantation system and its effects on local life, right from the colonial beginnings of the region.

Between 1492 and the last shipments of enslaved Africans to the Caribbean region, around the end of the Civil War in the United States, that region is thought to have received somewhere between a third and a half of all of the slaves shipped to the New World. Given the modest size of the colonies involved, this suggests how astonishingly intense and utterly deadly were the slave economies of the region. Recent estimates, based on fuller and more complete records of the trade, provide an even more somber picture. In his most recent book, Rediker (2007:4–7) gives a brief, sobering précis of New World slavery and its consequences. Nearly twelve and a half million Africans were shipped to the New World, he tells us, of whom nearly two million died en route. Most of those arriving alive became plantation slaves. Another three million died in Africa, in the period between their capture and the boarding of the slave ships; and nearly a million and a half more would die in their first year in the New World. He writes, chillingly: "Another way to look at the loss of life would be to say that an estimated 14 million people were enslaved to produce a 'yield' of nine million longer-surviving enslaved Atlantic workers."

The Caribbean islands were critically important in this picture, both as entrepots for the trade and as recipients of a disproportionate part of the human cargoes shipped westward. But not all of the islands were important in the trade at the same time; there were highs and lows in the delivery of their chained cargoes; and some of the islands participated little or not at all in the centuries-long plantation frenzy. For those that did, a lasting mark was left. Jamaica, which is about twice the size of Delaware, disembarked an estimated one million enslaved Africans. The French colony of Saint Domingue, a bit larger than Maryland, received a few more than three-quarters of a million, before the Haitian Revolution (Eltis and Richardson 2008:49, 51).[12] When slavery ended in Jamaica, emancipation created about 310,000 freed persons; and on the eve of the Haitian Revolution, French Saint Domingue had about 450,000 slaves. In neither place had the slaves successfully reproduced themselves, and the numbers of those alive when freedom came suggest how deadly slavery proved to be to its victims. Rogozinski (2000:140) calls the sugar plantation "a killing machine"; Hochschild (2005), writing of tea, calls it "the blood-sweetened beverage" because of the sugar with which it was sweetened. Brown's *Reaper's Garden*

(2008) is centered on the ghastly, many-sided relationship between the plantations and death.

Though there is an enormous literature dealing with the slavery era and the people who were its victims, something can still be said about its aggregate meaning for world history, and about its consequences for the descendants of the slaves. As an anthropologist, I think that the so-called peculiar institution of slavery was so critical in human history that it is also worth asking what it may signify for a general theory of human culture. In my view, the Caribbean slavery experience was unique in its implications for the nature of human social life. Perhaps anthropology can help to explain those implications.

I will defer that discussion until the last chapter. Here, however, I must address to anthropology's boundary with history. Many anthropologists seeking other approaches to our humanity have moved away from what we share with the discipline of history. I have always thought that doing anthropological fieldwork and then trying to integrate what one found out into the relevant local, regional, or national history was a useful and important task.

When we look at any aspect of social life in these three societies, we find that their noticeably different social and economic histories go along with (and may help to explain) significant differences in the way people conceive of themselves, and cling to (or change) their values. In what follows, I wish to draw out some of those similarities and differences by calling on the people I have known to "testify," so to speak. In turning to them for material, of course, I privilege them beyond all of those persons I did not come to know so well. These "testifiers" were almost without exception ordinary people. By "ordinary" I mean working people, people who own little, and mostly work with their hands.[13] I add that they were also uneducated and poor, and could do very little for their children (though some of them tried awfully hard to do more). Those I mention were also mostly rural—manual laborers who had been physically strong and inured to crippling labor, but also prone to illness, lacking decent medical care, and not likely to live long lives. They lived in poor countries with unpromising futures, almost as unpromising for their children as for them.

These are countries with colonial pasts that have remained singularly difficult to overcome. Among their legacies were social systems that left little room for expanding economic opportunities, and few resources for more training, even for those motivated to seek it. By contrast, and since about World War II, we North Americans have not reflected enough about the rich opportunities for training and education that so many of us matter-of-factly enjoy. Our unawareness has the undesirable effect of coarsening our understanding of the relationship between opportunity and ability. Many of us have difficulty remembering to what extent our individual performances turned ultimately upon wider opportunities that actually have relatively little to do with individual character and virtues. We run the risk of putting too high a value on our individual performances, because we ignore the wider social conditions that made our successes easier to achieve.

The triumphs of a V. S. Naipaul or a Derek Walcott or a W. Arthur Lewis—all Nobel laureates from the British West Indies—should not blind us to just how terrible are the odds against any such single success in their regions of origin. When those odds are compared with the odds in, say, a country such as Canada or the United States, it seems remarkable that anyone succeeds in the

Caribbean. All these persons achieved their successes partly by leaving the lands of their birth. There are people like Kamau Brathwaite and George Lamming, who were successful abroad and then came back home to the islands. But their successes should not mislead us about the difficulties that the battered social systems and frail economies of these former colonial societies impose upon their children when they seek education, fame, and fortune—no matter how hard they work.

People of the sort who figure in what follows do not live outside great events but within them. And because great events do not become great without the participation of the people, the people themselves are made great by the events they collectively bring into being. Any told life is likely to include an account of a great event, but seen from a distinctive, individual perch. That is something that great oral-historical storytellers, such as Studs Terkel, fully appreciate. They know that it took countless persons, millions of them suffering or dying, to make the great event called World War II. It was by their acts that they made that event great, and thereby that they became great themselves. When one such person recounts her experiences, the event "behind" her life could be a natural disaster, a depression, or a war. In the telling, few narrations treat any such event as other than happenstance or an act of God: circumstances such as the weather or the seasons or "fate."

Many great events lack the immediacy and peril of a hurricane or a battle. Some institutions with long histories, such as slavery, have an everydayness, an acquired familiarity for those who endured them, that thins out or conceals the ways in which they were paramount (and often horrific). Such institutions are not really "events." They are more like whole fragments or strips of social fabric, punctured by events and then remended. So for most of us, slavery in the U.S. South can mostly be grasped as background for the Civil War. Unfortunately, this way of seeing slavery was encouraged by literature and, soon enough, by cinema. Accordingly, the institution of slavery itself or the events of the Civil War seemed to need no description; they were simply the canvas on which individual lives—generals, widows, soldiers (rarely slaves)—might be painted as self-portraits.

Weaving the spoken memories and thoughts of "little people" into the history of events and institutions is not easy to do. The testimony is often of a kind that tells us how events or institutions have shaped—and damaged—individual lives. But the narrators mostly tell us what happened to *them*. "World War II" or "slavery" are not subjects that most persons talk about as such. Each talks instead about what happened to her (or him); the larger events can be death, a hurricane, a war, background to the memory of pain or joy of personal experience. The persons I will quote and paraphrase here perceive this way, for the most part; only rarely do they lift their eyes to the larger canvases.

But what they say lets us see how experience and the wider world lie next to each other in the consciousness of the narrator. Such articulated memories also afford us a different take on past and present. Recounting an event from long ago, the speaker draws on memory to compose a story; often it is in the timbre and volume of voice that we hear (if we are listening) how the past is summoned. If we are fortunate, it may help us get a notion of history that we can only rarely produce for ourselves—unless it is a story that we ourselves are telling.

My hope is that the interweaving of larger canvas and individual voice will let us see better how each illuminates the other.[14] I am drawing in large measure on my field notes about what people were like, about what they said and meant. Yet in spite of a lifetime spent largely in the study of the Caribbean region, my grasp of the character of the societies and peoples that compose it is by no means as confident as I would like. There are many different societies, all of them with lengthy and variegated histories. Though generalizations about the region are common, they are mostly platitudes and paraphrases. Change—at times rapid, other times slow—has obviously never ceased. Oddly, becoming more familiar with any one place actually makes it harder to generalize, not easier.

There is also always the question of how one is trained to learn, and how best to communicate what one has discovered. Anthropological training heavily influences my sense of how one sets out to learn about a country and its people, even though I know now that when I began, I was not very aware of it. Many of us anthropologists used to work in a characteristic way, staying a long time in just one place that was strange or new to us, usually getting to know truly well only a handful of persons in that place. They were likely to be persons of the sort commonly called "the man in the street," or "ordinary people." I tried to do that in several different places, and most of what I write here is about friends I made who lived in those three pieces of the Antillean mosaic that I came to know best. I hope that what I learned by listening and watching in these places will enable me to clarify something about each of them, in a somewhat larger way.

And so this book deals with the three Antillean societies in which I carried out most of my New World fieldwork, and with the knowledge of some of the individuals in each society whom I came to know personally during the time I spent in their home villages. About the three societies themselves—Jamaica, Haiti, and Puerto Rico—I offer a few historical observations. These three share broad similarities that stem from their geography, the parts they played in the development of European overseas power, and the social histories of their populations. All were settled by European colonists and enslaved Africans; in all, native peoples were mostly killed off by disease and enslavement; into all, and over long stretches of time, large numbers of enslaved Africans were dragged. Again in all three, there was much cultural as well as biological intermixture. In all three—and this seems to me far more important than simple borrowing or mixing of cultural materials—there was considerable building of ways to live, a building of cultural systems. Thus I deal here with places whose histories were broadly alike in many important ways, but they were certainly not by any means interchangeable. These were societies that differed, and differ greatly, among themselves, even in the place of slavery in their history, or in their historical demography.

It is important to determine at what levels of generality similar histories make peoples alike. In the societies I describe here, there were (and are) many physical and social features that are peculiar to each. Those differences can actually help to make comparisons among them more illuminating. If on the one hand what they have in common enables us to claim that there is a group or class of similar societies that we can call "the Caribbean region," those features should serve as a baseline for comparisons. If on the other hand they are different enough from each other to let us see their distinctive characteristics contrastively, then looking at them a little more closely may tell us something about the relation between particular causes and effects. The social consequences of centuries of slavery, for example, are to some extent the same in each case. Yet each case can throw light on other cases by virtue of its distinctive features. This might help us grasp more firmly how one outcome came to be different from another.

Here is an example, one that figures importantly in what follows. Puerto Rico was settled early after its conquest, and though slaves were brought there from the start, the majority population came to be European-descended and free, while the native (Indian) population was killed off rapidly by maltreatment and disease, or absorbed into the wider genetic pool.[15] In later centuries as the economic importance of the slaves dwindled, the free population rose, and the physical appearance of the majority became more mixed. In the nineteenth century, when the demand for slaves rose sharply, it was no longer possible for the sugar producers to import as many slaves as they wanted. By then, Puerto Rico had developed a large, free, physically mixed, landless population. The colonial leaders, together with landowners keen to expand production, hit on a remarkable solution to their "labor problem": to force landless inhabitants of whatever appearance to work alongside the slaves on the plantations. They were able to get legislative approval from Spain's government to coerce their poorer fellow citizens to work. Many of those free but coerced landless workers were of mixed ancestry; many were, by the familiar standards of North Americans, phenotypically white.[16] Only in this single Caribbean case was such an arrangement imposed on local people.[17] I believe that this historical experience made Puerto Rico unique in its race relations and in its racial attitudes, and that much of that heritage has been perpetuated—

though I must add quickly that it is in no sense the same as the absence of racism.

Such historically determined differences "explain" in a particular manner. Sociocultural patterns—such as particular ways of thinking about gender, or "race," or who is "family," or what is insulting—take on their shape in accord with specific conditions. When we can say something about where the continuity of social events leads us, we sharpen our ability to grasp how opinions form, and then how they harden or soften in gear with other events, and with the passage of more time. The past continually conditions the present, of course, and it does so through attitudes and beliefs and laws that express and embody the past, even when no explicit reference to the past is part of them. People in the United States who argue—angrily—over the public recognition of the Confederate flag need not invoke the past for us to know that in their anger the past is present.[18] Each past, of course, once *was* the present, and our present will one day be but another past. But some parts of the past are endowed with astonishing vitality because the living validate those parts, reenact them, regret them. In one way or in many, the past is in their heads, there to be drawn on, acknowledged or not. In the case of the Caribbean region, that is also true. The past is always there, though in the Caribbean, few statues or battlefields or cemeteries serve as reminders.[19]

Not all anthropologists agree with my perspective on these things. Many see the aims of anthropology as different. I continue to be interested in trying to figure out what, and who, made things happen; to what extent they succeeded or failed in doing so; what the consequences were for those who had to live (or die) with the outcomes. Rebecca Scott, whose comparisons of the post-Emancipation struggles in Cuba and Louisiana (1985, 2005) have greatly enhanced our understanding of historical processes, thinks that instead of "factors" or "causes," the concept of "freedom" must be parsed, in order to judge in what ways, and how much, different societies failed or succeeded in giving to freedom the meanings former slaves imagined it to encompass. I think her goal—addressed impressively by her books—is a more ambitious and exacting one than my own. What I attempt here, I think, is more modest. I do try to make my own sense out of the past. I also want to give some picture of the people with whom I lived and worked. Their perceptions, as I recorded them, throw some personal and individual light, I think, on the past that they and their ancestors experienced, day by day.

Of course there is no one explanation for what are in reality complex series of events. Anthropologists can try—as do some historians—to figure out why such a series of events took one course rather than another. The answers, of course, are contingent. History only looks inevitable after the fact; students of history understandably avoid inevitability as an explanation of anything. Contingent answers are based on the way different pertinent factors are weighed by the interpreter when making judgments. Hence the study is of how to weigh the effect of one or another group or law or event historically, when looking at a particular outcome. The answers may convince no one, but I think they are worth looking for, all the same.

It was once said that anthropology would one day have to choose between being history and being nothing at all. Then, for a period of several decades, many American cultural anthropologists were under the spell of a British view that considered history largely irrelevant to the practice of anthropology. That period is long passed.

Now the relationship is cordial, sometimes even intimate; but the two fields still differ substantially. Anthropologists differ from historians for what are mostly methodological reasons; some differences are obvious. Historians study the past, whereas ethnographers usually deal with contemporary people and events. Anthropologists who are interested in historical questions will more likely have living sources for some of their knowledge, in part because they are more accustomed to live in the places where they study and in part because historians usually do not need living informants for their theoretical ideas. And when settling down to work, there is some space between what historical anthropologists and historians do. We both use the library, as well as primary sources, if those exist; we both ponder how something happened without being able to watch it happen;[20] and we're both likely—especially these days—to visit the places where it happened. We may be equally disposed to learn the language people speak there,[21] become friends with the people there, or bother these new friends in search of clues about what happened long ago. Still, the historians may differ from anthropologists in the professional opportunities afforded them to do those things or the professional incentives to do them.[22]

Since the relation between particular postulated or supposed causes and particular effects is a proper source of argument, I hope by what I write here to raise some issues, even if I do not have any entirely convincing answers. These issues have to do with such things as what happened to people culturally when they were enslaved; whether what I call a "peasant way of life" was ever possible for New World peoples after they were freed from slavery; and what in the history of race and gender relations in Jamaica, Haiti and Puerto Rico might be relevant to the present. But such questions won't be "answered" here. This book is mostly a meditation, a personal look back—not weighty scholarship. Still, I hope by what I write here to make the questions I ask better ones.

The work I draw on here I did as a ethnographer and amateur historian. For an anthropologist to claim that what he or she learned from half a dozen people in a country is somehow collectively representative of that country's culture would be ludicrous. Yet I think it is a worthwhile effort to try to conjoin some distinctive features of the past in each country with what some people there had said to me in response to my questions, or with the behavior of some whom I had been able to listen to or observe. Anthropologists differ from historians. But they also work differently from reporters, novelists, soldiers, missionaries, physicians, traders. I hope to make clear here what it is that some ethnographers do to perceive and understand that makes their work different from that of other observers and witnesses such as missionaries or soldiers.

A casual traveler to these or other islands of the Caribbean region would notice all sorts of likenesses among them—the almost inescapable sun; the sometimes torrential rains; the lush vegetation, often starkly contrasted with bare bedrock; in most places, the nearness of the sea; the arid expanses of stony farmland, damaged by overuse and mining; the all too common poverty; the wonderful music, as pervasive as the sunshine; the variegated appearance of the people, and the rainbow spectrum of "nonwhiteness" among them. European and American cities have now taken on some of that once startling variety and color. But in the Caribbean, it is the way people have looked for a very long time.

In the countryside one sees how they live in little roadside strips—what the Germans call *Strassendörfen*—but also in clusters.

High in the hills, one sees them living in some places in scattered tiny houses. One might notice the fruit vendors at the crossroads, the palm trees, the thick, graceful, featherlike groves of tall bamboo shimmering in the brilliant sunshine, and the lizards and land crabs—possibly even the little that is left in most places today of the cane fields, or the ruined chimneys of now-extinct grinding mills. All of these things the three islands share. They share as well their general location—tropical, marine, insular—though they differ from most of the islands around them in their size, among other things.

Jamaica is about 4,400 square miles, Puerto Rico about 3,400; and Haiti, the western third of the island Columbus named Española (Santo Domingo), about 11,000 square miles. The only larger island neighbor is Cuba, which lies to the west of Española and Puerto Rico and north of Jamaica: 44,000 square miles. The western end of Cuba lies just ninety miles south of the Florida Keys and the same distance east of the northern shores of Mexico's Yucatán peninsula. From the mouth of the Gulf of Mexico in the west, it extends eastward some seven hundred miles. These four islands make up the Greater Antilles. From Puerto Rico, the easternmost of these big islands, their little island neighbors lie mostly in a great eastward-bending arc strung all the way south to Trinidad, off the coast of Venezuela—nearly 1,000 miles. There are many outliers—three Dutch islands off Venezuela's coast; two tiny Colombian islands in the Gulf of Mexico; and others here and there. All together, they compose the Lesser Antilles.

Experts agree that Columbus's first landfall was in the Bahamas. He then proceeded to discover the islands to their south—the Greater and Lesser Antilles.[23] Until 1519, when Cortés landed in Mexico and

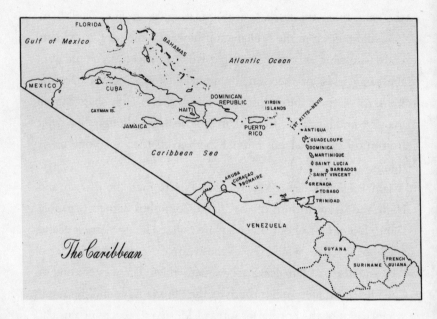

The Caribbean.

From Sidney W. Mintz and Sally Price, eds., *Caribbean Contours*
(Baltimore: Johns Hopkins University Press, 1985:2); used by permission.

marched inland, the Caribbean islands were mostly what Europe assumed the New World to be. And for a long time, some thought they were part of Asia.

The dominant economic features of European rule in the Caribbean colonies were slavery as the source of labor and the plantation as the instrument of production. There was slavery in Jamaica under the Spaniards, but slavery became important there only after the British seized it in 1655. Santo Domingo was also Spanish. After its western third was ceded to France in 1697 and became Saint Domingue, slavery became important there. In both places the rise of the plantation system depended on slave labor. In Puerto Rico, though the first slaves were brought within two decades of settlement, if not earlier, slave importation was scanty and intermittent, at least until near the middle of the nineteenth century. Only then did slaves became economically more important there, and never as important as in the others.

Slavery ended in Puerto Rico in 1873. But there, as in other parts of the region, the end of slavery didn't equal emancipation. An "apprenticeship" system was quickly installed, and the supposedly free "apprentices" were actually not free until 1876. By the time slavery ended there, its economic importance had dwindled; and though it had never been as important there as in Jamaica and Saint Domingue, its social effects were real. When slavery ended in Jamaica (and throughout the British West Indies) in 1833–34, there, too, it was followed by "apprenticeship."[24]

In Haiti (Saint Domingue), slavery ended definitively in 1804 when Haiti became an independent nation after its Revolution. There was a fragile earlier emancipation under French revolutionary rule (1793–94). But the invading British, until 1798, suppressed that law in the areas of Saint Domingue under their control. Napoleon hoped to revoke emancipation but never succeeded. In the end, the Haitian rebels defeated the French invaders, and in 1804 Haiti became the New World's second nation.

Whereas the populations of Jamaica and French Saint Domingue (Haiti) were to become preponderantly African in origin over the centuries, that was not the case in Puerto Rico. And whereas Jamaica would add people from India, China, and elsewhere, that was to be far less the case in Puerto Rico and in Haiti. Hence, not only the institution of slavery itself varied in duration and significance in these islands; the physical composition of the local population and the importance and influence of groups of freed and nonwhite persons in each also changed through time, lending distinctive character to each society.

The growing or waning importance of slavery was of course tied to local economic conditions, island by island. Ultimately in all three it was tied to metropolitan politics as well. Slaves were imported above all in order to supply labor for the production of commodities of growing economic significance in Europe. I have noted elsewhere (Mintz 1985) that sugar, coffee, tea, and chocolate became especially significant in the diets of the European working classes, due to their stimulant (and because of the sugar, caloric) value. All except for tea figured importantly in Caribbean economic growth, and the three colonies of interest here played important parts in that story. Sugar was added to all three beverages in Europe—in each case, a European innovation. In those centuries the Caribbean colonies were famed for their sugar and its appetizing derivative products molasses and rum. Coffee, cacao, and other crops followed behind, especially coffee—but in the Caribbean, coffee production never became as large in scale as that of sugar. Mostly coffee was cultivated on small holdings, often by family labor, with or without a few slaves.

Sugar, however, and its related byproducts, molasses and rum, were produced on large agricultural estates—plantations—that relied primarily on slave labor from their beginnings, as early as the 1500s, until the end of Caribbean slavery (in Cuba) in 1886. Over time, there were other forms of coercion, and other sources of labor besides Africa. As I've suggested, slavery itself varied in significance in different Caribbean locales during nearly four full centuries. Nonetheless, the Caribbean region has been *defined* by both the enslavement of Africans and the production of sugar and its byproducts on large plantation enterprises.

In British Jamaica and French Saint Domingue slave labor drove the economy, and these two locales, by virtue of their production, their slave numbers, and their importance to their respective metropolises, represented climaxes of the plantation system in the eighteenth century. Where that system was strong, slavery usually tended to drive away or discourage the use of free labor.[25] The economies of Jamaica and Saint Domingue were cases where plantations, the planter class, and slave labor dominated the functioning of the whole society. Yet before the mid-nineteenth century the system itself was repeatedly challenged, from the beginning by revolt from below and later by both local and homeland reformists from above. In 1804, the sovereign nation of Haiti took form, put an end to the colonial plantation system, and made clear that legal slavery would not return. In Jamaica in 1838 and, to a much lesser extent, in Puerto Rico in 1876, the colonial regimes faced the problem of replacing the slaves in the local economies, once slavery ended.

After freedom came, in Jamaica the plantation lived on, weakened; in Haiti it disappeared. In Puerto Rico, the end of slavery had relatively less serious consequences. The slaves had been a smaller proportion of the total population. And when they became free, they were mainly tied to the local estates by lack of economic alternatives, the three-year apprenticeship laws, and the connivance of local officials (Figueroa 2005).

As I have indicated there had been an uneven but significant inflow of European migrants to Puerto Rico. The importation of African slaves, minor in Puerto Rico in comparison to Jamaica and Saint Domingue, was similarly uneven. Because the plantation economy in Puerto Rico developed feebly and intermittently and over so long a time, slaves there were often freed, or were able to purchase their freedom (Figueroa 2005:79–104). In the sixteenth and seventeenth centuries most Puerto Ricans were poor, rural, and uninvolved in producing anything for export. There was considerable mixing of people of differing ancestries, and relatively little institutional regulation of social life outside the island's principal city.

This description does not apply to what French Saint Domingue and Jamaica became, because of differences in the era of settlement and in the rates and types of economic development. Nonetheless, these three societies shared one feature that deeply affected the way they eventually turned out. It has to do with the plantation form itself, and how it did it (or did not) develop—specifically, the way those societies became a frontier of Europe, and the role the plantations played in that process.

The plantation system, particularly in the case of sugar, requires the installation of productive arrangements that embrace both field and factory. It is nature that determines such an intimate twinning of land and machines. Because sugarcane must be cut quickly when ripe to optimize sugar yield and ground quickly when cut to avoid spoilage and desiccation, successful sugarcane processing and sugar making comprise a highly time-sensitive activity, wedding field to factory. Especially during the lengthy harvest season of those times, any break in the chain of continuous effort could become an economic disaster. Workers had to be able to deal with sudden changes in the flow of cut cane to the mill; to stay active for endless hours, without sleep or food; above all, to respond to orders efficiently. The success of such close unity of field and mill turned on a completely malleable labor force. In the Caribbean region for several centuries, it was a slave labor force disciplined by the use of implacable violence. In the sixteenth century nothing like those plantation enterprises had ever been seen before by Europe.[26]

Though the plantations were depicted in later centuries almost as if they were feudal estates—the slave quarters as picturesque, the mills as centers of energetic cooperation overseen by stern (but benign) masters—the truth was infinitely harsher. The plantations were governed by violence of every kind and at every level. The system's abuse and inhuman labor regime horrifically shortened and ended lives. When buying more slaves was cheaper than maintaining the lives of the slaves one had—and this was commonly remarked on—planters bought more slaves. There was nothing in the slightest picturesque about the plantations. They had almost no resemblance to feudalism or Greek slavery. They anticipated by centuries the quite different oppression that marked the Industrial Revolution. And they punished their victims with even greater impunity, in horrifying and often disgusting ways.

From the early sixteenth century until at least the mid-nineteenth, the colonial Caribbean was a key European economic region. Key economic regions rise and fall for technological, demographic, ecological, or political reasons as the larger systems of which they are parts change character. But the part any such regions play in larger systems is affected by the kind and degree of internal integration a region itself manifests. In the case of the New World in general, and specifically in the Caribbean, pioneering economic undertakings were enabled by the launching of national military, political, and economic initiatives in Europe and were then imposed on both native and introduced people, distant from the European epicenter. Enterprises in the Americas became frontiers for Europe.[27]

Edgar T. Thompson (1932) pointed out long ago that plantations—rather than being tropical institutions, as others had claimed—were above all frontier institutions.[28] "Plantation" once meant "settlement" (as in Plymouth Plantation), only acquiring over time the meaning of "agricultural estate" and later "tropical agricultural estate." In the Caribbean islands, with their native populations wiped out by disease and war, the plantations were implanted enterprises, manned with foreign (for centuries mostly enslaved) labor. Each served as a settlement focus in places the new settlers had emptied of people. Links between frontiers, slavery, and plantations made economic, if not moral, sense. In many thinly populated world regions in the sixteenth century land was cheap or free, and Europeans were land hungry.[29]

Plantations tended to grow first near the coasts of islands or along mainland littorals, from which the shipment of products both out and in was most economical. Native peoples were by then often killed off, driven off, or enslaved—if there were any left. In the absence of plentiful labor, not yet subject to any widespread moral judgment, slavery emerged as the "best" way to get work done. Often preceded by indentured labor and sometimes accompanied by, or followed by, contracted (and coerced but legally free) labor, slavery was for centuries the mainstay of the New World sugar plantations. Slaves were one kind of capital investment; their upkeep represented some long-term supply costs for the slaveholder. If they fell ill, or became too old to work, or were idle during economic downturns, it was less expensive to set them free than to keep them. This was often a factor in their being freed.

A complex aspect of the Caribbean plantation system, which flourished at different times both in large islands such as Cuba and small ones such as Martinique, was how it affected other parts of the local economy. In a society as large as Cuba—or one in which the slave plantation sector was relatively modest—a small-farm sector could flourish. But in places that came to rely primarily on slave labor and plantation production, little else in the local economy could grow, other than the plantations. In Jamaica, in the era of plantation growth, around 1730–1830, the population consisted in good measure of slaves, and the attorneys, accountants, managers and other free people who were needed to keep the slaves working and the plantations running. In the Caribbean, free small farmers usually had trouble when they had to compete with the plantations for land, labor, or anything else. In Barbados, a small island, when the British colonists turned to sugar, the small farmers were eventually driven out entirely for lack of land.

Without small farmer communities, the need for masons, carpenters, blacksmiths, wheelwrights, and most other craftsmen was mostly limited to the plantations, which soon came to train and use slaves for these purposes. Except as places for import-export activities, for fulfilling the needs mainly of soldiers and sailors, and as government seats, Caribbean towns lacked much basis on which to grow.[30] From the seventeenth century almost until the middle of the nineteenth—except for the Hispanic islands, and those too small, too dry, or too mountainous to be suitable plantation locales—the plantations were often the predominant institution.

Yet the societies formed by the people who lived outside the plantation system were entirely different from the plantation itself. On the large islands, and to a lesser extent even on the small ones, the contrast between the plantations as important economic enterprises and the rest of the local society was also that of economic center versus some sort of frontier—in the larger islands, economic centers versus internal frontiers. By the seventeenth century—again excepting the Spanish colonies—Caribbean islands were relatively empty of settlement, their native peoples dead or absorbed genetically into the settler population. Hence, most of the people who inhabited the islands who were not connected to the plantations were "frontiersmen," in one way or another: runaway slaves, squatter farmers, army deserters, pirates, fisher folk, ranchers, and vagabonds.[31] I must be careful with what I claim. I have qualified these assertions by reference to the large islands first settled by Spain—Cuba, Puerto Rico, and Santo Domingo—which had developed, in their first colonial centuries, rural populations of this kind, whose attachments to the metropolis lost their significance (if, indeed, they had developed any). These were the people who thought of themselves as native and, to be sure, many of them were partly of Native American origin. But in none of these three places did there develop an enduring sugar industry, with slaves and plantations, before the mid-eighteenth century. By contrast, on the island colonies of the other European powers, it was plantation growth that led to population, and those populations were overwhelmingly of African origin and enslaved.

I mean to suggest that, by their nature, plantations do not stimulate the growth of agricultural hinterlands producing surpluses that the state can tax or that warlords can exact. Moreover, these were societies chronically lacking enough police or militia (laws requiring militia service were common, and gave special meaning to issues of racial equality among the free). In a society such as Jamaica, an important reason for going into the countryside and away from the towns or plantations was slave-catching. Typically, these were also societies in which manual labor was stigmatized as work only for slaves. Small towns were outposts of the state, and because of slavery, the colonial state was to a large extent a policing and coercing institution in the Caribbean rather than a means of institutionalizing other state functions (such as religion, law, or education).

Yet the plantations, which witnessed scenes of awful cruelty and backbreaking labor, were nonetheless often like oases for the resident Europeans, existing as they did in a largely uninhabited landscape. In places like Jamaica and French Saint Domingue the mountains, in places like the mainland coastal Guianas the interior forests, and even on the smaller islands the mangrove swamps and more remote areas were for centuries frontiers for people who were bent on escaping the plantations and state power—especially but not only the *cimarrones,* the so-called maroons or runaway slaves.

The importance of these circumstances to the larger story rests in the distinctive plantation-countryside imbalance: developed and undeveloped, the tame and the wild, the "civilized" and "uncivilized." Yet from a European perspective, the plantations themselves, frontier institutions based on violence, could be seen as undeveloped, wild, and uncivilized. To speak, then, of "a key economic region" when referring to the Caribbean certainly does not mean that these islands were built socially in the form of European societies.

The plantation societies were divided socially and economically in ways that made them qualitatively different from the nations of Europe. Most of the Europeans living in Jamaica and French Saint Domingue were not there to stay. Though there were exceptions, few seemed to conclude that Jamaica or Saint Domingue was a safe and agreeable place in which to settle down for life. In inescapable contrast to them, their neighbors in these colonies were the enormous populations of *enslaved* people—impoverished, undernourished, lacking all legal rights. Most of those people most of the time not only were suffering but also acutely aware of the source of their misery.

From the European perspective, the Caribbean colonies were backwaters in every respect, except for the wealth that they produced. European officials and scholars understood from afar that what they perceived as backwardness was closely linked to the fact that their populations were not only not European, in origins or in culture, but also enslaved. Though there was peddled in Europe the planter view that the slaves lived decent and fulfilling lives, and were actually being saved and improved in a state of slavery, the question of why, in that case, slavery was necessary became over time less and less rhetorical.

Among free people in Saint Domingue and Jamaica meanwhile, slavery was clearly recognized as the keystone institution of their present, and even more important, future economic security. They knew well that Caribbean social and political life rested in the hands of the planters; and the planters were the largest slaveholders and the fiercest defenders of slavery. That the institution which underlay the accumulating wealth of a tiny free minority was also the cause of the misery and suffering of the enormous unfree majority was a contradiction of huge—no doubt at times even terrifying—proportions.

One has to ask what the social norms must have been like in a society in which most people saw themselves either as robbed of their own lives and stolen from their homelands or as pursuing a disagreeable, coarse, and even dangerous, if sometimes lucrative, duty far from home. Of course, over time many Caribbean people came to believe that, for them, where they were *was* home. Modest success with ranching, small farms, and trade on the Hispanic islands was not threatened by the growth of large plantations, with their armies of slaves, until the nineteenth century. Spanish colonists and their descendants there soon began to feel as if they belonged where they were (Giusti-Cordero 2009, Mintz 1967). One early scholar (Wright 1916) pointed out that, by the early sixteenth century, the people in Cuba, Puerto Rico, and Santo Domingo had kinsmen whom they knew in most of the other island settlements. But only in a few places, slowly and painfully, did a sense of truly being Caribbean, rather than European, begin to take shape. It seems pretty clear that such a sense of belonging does not affect everyone at the same rate, or even for the same reasons, and that people who do not come to feel that way may have different reasons for it.

One of the complicating factors was—of course—what is called "race." On many islands, the arrival of numerous Africans and few Europeans meant that differences in appearance would become indexed with who one was and how much wealth and power one had, or lacked. Such differences can militate powerfully against a sense of common identity or belonging—especially big differences in privilege. Indeed, as Burnard (2004) points out, the communities of whites and of blacks were made more separate and at the same time internally more coherent by the way "race" was perceived.

We see before us, then, a group of small colonial societies that had their beginnings in the first decades of the sixteenth century, all under Spanish rule, and then were thrust into far more trying histories by the swift growth of northern European rivalry with Spain throughout the region after about 1625. In the case of the big islands, where Spain first put settlers, the frantic search for gold resulted in little, except the nearly total destruction of native peoples. After Cortés reached Mexico in 1519, settlers in the islands learned of the large native mainland populations, the abundant land, and the great mineral wealth, and many left for the mainland. Still only sparsely populated by Europeans in the sixteenth century, places like Cuba and Puerto Rico actually lost population for some time, intensifying the contrast in those islands between the internal frontier and the few loci of insular colonial settlement. Before the eighteenth century, Spain was not much interested in local economic development in her Caribbean colonies. But with the Danes, the Dutch, the English, the French, and others that development was soon to come.

I have stressed to what an extent successful settlement came to depend on plantations, slave labor, and goods desired in Europe. After the mid-seventeenth century, slaves were brought in larger and larger numbers to the northern European plantation colonies. But in places like Puerto Rico, Cuba, and Santo Domingo, enslaved—

and frequently freed—Africans, and then their descendants, had been present almost from the beginnings of colonial settlement. What happened to these populations culturally—that is, what languages they spoke, what systems of kinship they used, what cuisines they cooked, what music they sang—is anthropologically important. Much ink has been spilled in examining these issues. I will be brief here and say more later.

Except for the Native Americans, obviously everyone in the New World came from elsewhere or was descended from someone who did. In the northern colonies, many of the newcomers came in groups from the same place and speaking the same language, many even sharing the same faith. Much of the material of their daily life they had carried with them. But even these newcomers were unable to retain every object, practice, and belief. In their new homes they were obliged to eat new foods, adjust to somewhat different seasons, deal with new plants and animals in a new setting, and live among peoples dramatically different from themselves in appearance, language, and behavior.

The perpetuation of culture to some extent always depends on *place*. In the Caribbean region, the favorite Spanish food sources— wheat, olives, almonds, grapes—were not successfully grown. Churches were faithfully built; but all but a few of the priests were far away. Slowness of communication, dealing with culturally different people, different ecologies, all of it at unimaginable remoteness from home, meant that change was inescapable.

But if this was the case for the Europeans, it was equally so for the enslaved. The success of the slaves in building their own new cultures in spite of the everyday conditions they faced was a demonstration of their humanity. I have noted my belief that their cultural achievement may be unique in human history. That is a large claim. It rests, I think, on the way in which the slavery institution was founded and perpetuated, especially in those societies—the Caribbean islands, Brazil, and the Atlantic coast between—devoted primarily to the plantation production of sugar, molasses, and rum. A number of features worked together, I believe, in the formation and perpetuation of sugar plantation slavery: the nature of sugarcane, the arrangements for its production and the processing of the yield, the living arrangements, and the conditions of slave recruitment and enslavement. But rather than say more of these issues here, I will return to the three societies in which I did my work, and with which this book is mainly concerned.

Within each of these three Antillean societies, I had started with a particular problem, or set out to answer a question, having to do with rural life and social history. In all three cases I'd hoped that what I found out might throw light on some things bigger than the question itself. In Jamaica, I looked at what had been church-founded peasant villages. Many had been established after emancipation, and even before I visited Jamaica I had read about the one to which I later went. I wanted to find out how its community character could have been shaped by the way it had come into existence. But choosing that question meant I had also to ask whether villages that began in that way really differed from other kinds of villages in the same society.

In Haiti, I planned to study rural market women, to learn about their occupational training, how they conducted their businesses, and how they fit within Haiti's national economy. I was struck by Haiti's functioning as a nation, when it seemed to have hardly any national institutions—though I will have to explain later what I mean by that. And in Puerto Rico—where to some extent the boundaries of my field task had already been prescribed by the team project I was part of—I studied workers on a sugar plantation, to learn about local daily life and the economic and cultural forms that U.S. imperialism had taken after the military conquest of that society.

It had been while I was in Puerto Rico, the first of the three societies in which I worked, that I made a decision to tackle in subsequent years four culturally different Antillean societies as part of my emerging ambition to get a grasp of the region as a whole. I thought that there were four major imperial traditions in the region—Spanish, British, French, and Dutch[32]—and vowed to get to know at least a little about each of them. Up to the last, I nearly succeeded.

What I hope to do in this book is somewhat different from my original intentions when I worked in these places. Almost from the start, I have looked at the Caribbean as a region made coherent by its geography, climate, and terrain and also by particular features of a largely common history. That history was built on its tropical location, its mostly insular nature, and its early conquest by the Europeans. It was the region's suitability for "development" by means of slavery and a plantation system, and emergent world capitalism's readiness to batten on the needs and desires of the peoples of the conquering nations, that made its colonization such an enormous European success.

I argue at the same time that some of the differences *among* the three societies in which I worked can be attributed to their distinctive social character, even when we take into account regional historical commonality. But that raises a different question. What would lead anthropologists—as opposed to historians, or sociologists, or economists, say—to study village communities within large, complex, westernized societies of this sort? It is a fair question, given that anthropology had been concerned—almost to the very day I went to Puerto Rico with my fellow students—with the exclusive study of so-called primitive societies.

Without writing too much on a subject I have looked at elsewhere (Mintz 1977), I should mention that except for archeology, physical anthropology and folklore, anthropology had mostly ignored or disdained the Caribbean region until after World War II, mainly because its peoples were not—to use that once popular term—"primitives." Exactly because Caribbean history was filled with European aims and intentions from so early a time, anthropologists were not interested in it. The ideal society for study according to the profession's values in, say, 1940, was almost the logical opposite of a Caribbean society.

Most anthropologists sixty years ago thought places like Jamaica or Puerto Rico were simply imperfect artifacts of Western design. Their social organization was in the form of groups based on economic class, race, and individual property rather than kinship, friendship, religious role, or local villages or bands. Their economies were capitalistic, though they often exhibited what looked like unimportant little noncapitalist corners. The kinship systems of the laboring classes were thought to be incomplete, rudimentary, and deviant; their languages defective or "baby talk," their peoples "mongrelized." With few local exceptions, all of those islands seemed to lack three sociological features (quite spurious ones at that) that were important to anthropology even if its practitioners have never been willing to admit it: "purity," isolation, and romance.

Those anthropologists who did study the Caribbean region found it interesting, but instead of inspiring reverence for antiquity or purity, the islands and their surrounding shores looked at once tinsel-new and anciently tattered. A sinologist colleague who worked there one summer told me afterward that there was simply "no smell at all" of historical depth. And an eminent Caribbean writer notes—justifiably—that the region is typified by "an absence of ruins." Only one North American anthropologist before the 1940s, Melville Herskovits (1930), seemed to have thought the study of Caribbean peoples might illuminate important issues in the study of culture, abstractly conceived, or to provide theoretical insights, despite its culturally many-stranded history.

One reason it may be good to bring this into view now, though I have said most of it before (Mintz 1996), is that the last two decades have been marked by much excitement over the new ways the world is changing. The rhetoric about change is embodied in such terms as "globalization" and "creolization." These words are meant to stand for unprecedented transformations. I will comment on the extent to which I differ with these newer interpretations by suggesting that the concepts themselves, such as globalization and creolization, take on more meaning if one looks seriously at the Caribbean region. Globalization is not a new phenomenon; it is centuries old. Using "creolization" to describe supposedly global cultural processes implies that the Caribbean region, so long presumed to have nothing to teach anthropologists, is now thought to have much to teach them. Surprisingly, though, the Caribbean region and its own history have had hardly any role at all in this fashionable new rhetoric.[33]

2

Jamaica

THE CARIBBEAN is the oldest colonial region in modern Western history. Its conquest predates European control of most of the non-European world. Europe's earliest adventures in South Asia were about contemporary with the Hispanic Caribbean case, but most took longer to produce momentous results. To turn back to, say, the colonial outposts of the Italian city-states is to retreat too far from modernity.

Closer to the Caribbean colonies—indeed, linked to them historically—were the Canary Islands and Madeira. Together with some other islands and some enclaves in West Africa, these places fell within the pre-Columbian period of Luso-Hispanic expansion outside Europe. Historian Michael Zeuske (2006:173–264) has conceptualized a metaregion from the connections that arose between the islands of the Antilles and those of West Africa and the eastern Atlantic. He argues—justly, I think—that those links helped importantly to sustain the gradual rise of the Caribbean colonial economy, which would come to be built on slaves, plantations, and sugar. Zeuske's data suggest a world of multilingual and multiracial intermediaries, seamen, explorers, and businessmen carrying on their affairs in West Africa and the Caribbean and creating an "empire of islands." Here, however, I need to concentrate on the western Atlantic possessions themselves, and what became of them.

Within a couple of centuries the tiny Caribbean colonies assumed a major role, supplying once rare and costly tropical products to growing European markets. It was once common to refer to those goods as "dessert crops," but the phrase trivializes them and obscures the scale of overseas demand and buying power. From the sixteenth to the nineteenth centuries the global importance of such goods changed radically, and in Europe and elsewhere they became prosaic necessities even for the poor. In the last 150 years, the geography of their production has widened and the number of sweeteners offered for human consumption has multiplied. The effects of such changes on the Antillean island economies have been grave. Yet the global sweep of sugar and other sweeteners, now both non-caloric and caloric, remains immense. Here, I intend to look back mostly to the beginnings in the West.

Nowhere was the local impact of the rise of a sugar economy greater than in the island of Jamaica. From the infant beginnings of a plantation system there under the Spaniards in the sixteenth century through the British conquest in 1655 and right up to the end of slavery in 1834–38, the Jamaican plantation labor force was composed of enslaved Africans and their descendants. For nearly four whole centuries, slavery was an inescapable feature of Caribbean labor. In Jamaica as elsewhere in the region, and for the first time in the emerging modern world, people of differing physical type, culture, and social status were integrated into new social systems that, though established outside Europe, grew out of diverse European conceptions of political dependency. The Caribbean plantation prototype gave rise to arrangements of a sort that was then repeated in modified form in other parts of the larger regional complex known as "Afro-America," the "South Atlantic system," and now (more stylishly) "the Black Atlantic."[1]

I have said that what underlay that distinctive Caribbean development was above all the desire for sugar and the international rivalry for locales and labor power with which to supply it. Costly at first, but versatile, preservable and for nearly every consumer delicious, sucrose was an ideal commodity of modernity in late seventeenth-century Europe. As they grew plentiful and cheap, sugar, tobacco, and stimulant beverages became important symbols of rising capitalist practice and were the first desirable transoceanic commodities ever to be sold to masses of consumers. Newly marketed soft drugs such as cocoa, coffee, and tea became the constant companions of sugar.[2] Only tea did not end up being harvested in the tropical Americas.

For Europeans bent on investing in the New World plantations, sugar seemed like an inexhaustible source of great wealth. It supplied calories when consumed in hot, caffeine-rich drinks, supplementing such daily necessities as bread and cheese and gradually becoming part of everyday plebeian fare. The sugar plantations also reduced the costs to the European economies of feeding the growing masses of urban workers. The difference between the caloric yield of an acre of sugar—even under the conditions of its early production—compared to the caloric yield of an acre of cabbage, say, or even of wheat, was such that the advantages provided to the metropolitan economies by the successful partial substitution of sugar and the caffeine beverages for European staples were unexpectedly large.

Though it was Spain that pioneered sugarcane, plantations, and slaves in the Caribbean islands, Portugal was the European power that launched New World sugar production on a large scale—though not in the Caribbean. Portugal's colonial career in Brazil had been underwritten by a papal decree. Her resulting success in marketing in Europe was viewed with envy by the British, the French and, in particular, the Dutch. The Dutch had vied with the Portuguese in producing sugar on the South American mainland; but the Netherlands was unable to defend its first mainland colonies against Portugal's or, later, Britain's military power.

The British themselves had long been searching for tropical locations in which to produce sugar. Barbados, to which they laid claim around 1627, was their first real opportunity to do so. The first colonists there tried other crops before sugar and other labor forms before and alongside slavery, but with little success. They then got the help of sugar specialists, who came mostly from the small Dutch mainland colonies that had been overrun by the Portuguese. By the 1650s Barbados had become an immensely lucrative place, using African slaves to produce sugar for export to buyers of every class at home. Though at first there was hope in Britain of wresting the European sugar market from the Portuguese, Barbadian planters soon found that the British sweet tooth was almost insatiable, and the domestic market of the British isles—including Ireland, Wales, and Scotland—for a long time seemed almost infinite.

But Barbados was small—166 square miles—and its soils, flora, and fauna were brought under intense pressure (Watts 1987:219) by a booming economy that feverishly consumed soil, water, forest resources, and the lives of the slaves. In 1655 Admirals Penn and Venables, sent to the Caribbean by Cromwell as part of the Western Design, wrested Jamaica from Spain. Britain's overseas plantation system got an enormous boost. In under three decades Jamaica—more than 4,000 square miles larger than Barbados, rich in fertile alluvial flood plains, lush interior valleys, large forests, and ample water and untouched by European agricultural methods—had outstripped little Barbados.

Between about 1670 and 1808, Jamaica's plantation economy grew apace, becoming one of the most lucrative colonies in British colonial history. As I noted earlier, during those years a million enslaved Africans were dragged to Jamaica, the majority of them to work on the sugar plantations. The Jamaican economy therefore took on a character largely—but not entirely—defined by one crop, its social structure prevailingly integrated with the economy. A small but powerful planter class dominated both. Over time a similarly small and legally nearly powerless class of freed people of mixed ancestry took shape. This group was at first born of the rape of enslaved African women by Europeans in the colony. Some of their offspring were given or purchased their freedom.

After the first decades of British occupation, the Jamaican economy had become dominated by a plantation system based on slave labor and heavily committed to the production of sugar, molasses, and rum for export. The colony's entire governmental system was carried along by that economy. Very few slaves were freed, and the population of free people of color grew slowly before the nineteenth century. Free people became carpenters, masons, and tailors, and some were cultivators who sold their surpluses. They were concentrated in towns, especially Kingston, where they ran inns and small hotels, or worked as shipping clerks in the ports. Innkeepers, cooks, laundresses, and seamstresses were often free colored women; many had long-term relationships with white men. These persons filled important occupational niches, but few of them became wealthy, and practically none at first could exercise much influence in the colony's affairs.[3] Local law made it almost impossible for freed people to win anything resembling civil equality. Below these two small groups, and subject to them, there came to be many hundreds of thousands of slaves: captive Africans and the descendants of other captured Africans of past generations.

The social relations among these differing groups cannot be set apart from the sexual relations among them. In Jamaica as in all New World societies, the social and sexual together were aspects of how each such society took on its distinctive character. It may seem simplistic (or merely coarse) to say it—but seventeenth- and eighteenth-century Jamaica would have run more smoothly if the planters and their staffs had not become accustomed to raping female slaves with impunity. Indeed, many planters were aware of the adverse social consequences of such a pattern in daily life. But the hard fact is that they and their subalterns raped female slaves anyway.

At times this picture is allegedly softened by noting that some white men had long-term sexual relationships with their slaves, and at times freed their own children. I do not see how that makes the truth any softer. It surely did nothing for the legal status of non-whites as a group, nor did the show of parental protectiveness happen commonly. Most people in the planter class surely understood the social and ideological imprudence of creating a class made up of persons of mixed ancestry and limited rights who were the daughters and sons of the planters and their associates. Often the planters retained their children, together with their mothers, as their slaves. Certainly there were inspiring exceptions, but not so many as one might hope.[4] Keeping one's own wife and offspring as slaves struck numerous Europeans, even many English persons, as immoral, even—to use a word of the times—unnatural. Some Jamaicans, including relatives of the planters and many of the slaves, thought it was at least unseemly.[5] Slavery itself was considered moral by most white people, even by the few nonwhites who owned slaves. But it will surely be conceded that being a slave who is owned by one's own father conduces neither to filial piety nor to moral confidence in the social system under which one lives.[6]

Just as they do everywhere else, gender distinctions figure importantly in Jamaican history. But there they often blended into considerations of race as well. Plantation slavery, given the work regimen and the use of violence, tended to deemphasize sexual differences to a noticeable degree. In some ways male and female slaves were treated alike. Many of the Africans stolen from their natal villages and brought to Jamaica to be sold must already have learned culturally specific conceptions of themselves as males and females—as boys and girls, men and women. Capture and enslavement, the Middle Passage, and the discipline of the plantation surely wore away at those learned, culturally specific conceptions.

But people—even slaves and prisoners—have a profound need for social order, for normative practices that will enable them to live together and to interact. Though slavery meant abusive treatment for both its male and female victims, the slaves developed social codes of their own. Slavery nullified many former gender distinctions. But male and female slaves were perceived as different by planters and their subalterns during the course of daily life on the plantations. In allotting slaves to tasks, it was recognized that men were on average physically stronger than women. It was equally understood that women could be assaulted sexually and made to serve as mistresses and concubines and could bear children, who were born slaves. Though slavery removed some gender differences by leveling the treatment of the slaves in some regards, the social system that was created by the planters and colonial society in relation to the slaves reshaped gender differences and gave them a new form.

Social categories were developed by the overarching plantation order, particularly in regard to work.[7] Certain slaves were chosen to serve as gang bosses and drivers, coopers and smiths, domestic servants, nurses, coachmen, cooks, and watchmen. At the same time, some new role categories probably linked to emerging social and family life within the slave quarters, to religious practice, healing skills, personal counseling, and the like, were fashioned by the slaves themselves. Such different evolving categories did not merge easily with each other; slaves and their masters did not communicate freely.

Over time, plantation slavery also provided the raw material for the creation of social norms in regard to race. From the conquest of the island by Britain in 1655 onward, Jamaica's population was mostly British and African; as the plantation system succeeded economically, the proportion of people of African descent grew. By the time the plantations were at their apogee, the number of free whites and freed persons of mixed origin had also grown, but they remained modest fractions of the total population. Near the start of the nineteenth century some suggest Jamaica had about 35,000 free mixed and black persons, 30,000 whites, and a slave population of nearly 340,000.[8] Physical traits were quite tightly linked to social status. It seems highly probable that there were no phenotypically white persons who were slaves,[9] and no phenotypically black persons (though a few free colored, or whites of some African ancestry)[10] in the planter class (Hall 1972; Heuman 1981). Slight phenotypical differences were considered important for classifying individuals socially and over time only became more so. One did not have to be white in eighteenth-century Jamaica to be racially prejudiced. The deep personal feelings entangled with being classed as white or not white were strong, and in spite of all that has happened since, those feelings did not simply evaporate. In much of the Caribbean if not all, attitudes about color, the role of color in marking or validating status in a hierarchical system, the often obsessive preoccupation with how one looks in the spectrum of possibilities—these aspects of the perceived reality of physical variation certainly seem to have had enduring power.

I will not attempt to give any account here of the daily operation of Jamaican plantations in the past; the literature on these centers of colonial enterprise is very rich (e.g., Brathwaite 2005; Craton and Walvin 1970; Craton and Greenland 1978; Higman 1999, 2005). But one feature of the plantation system was tied so closely to the way the colony's rural sector developed that I want to describe it here. In the decades following Britain's seizure of Jamaica from Spain in 1655, relatively few small farms—called "pens"—developed that could produce foodstuffs for the plantations and the nonfarming free community. I say "relatively few" because of the strength of the plantation economy. Shepherd (2002) and her colleagues make clear that the nonsugar sectors of Jamaican rural life, particularly cattle and coffee producers, cannot be ignored. Even so, I think it is accurate to say that nearly all the food eaten in Jamaica from the seizure until emancipation either had to be imported for nearly everybody or else the slaves had to produce it. Planters were loath to use their slaves to grow food if this meant taking them away from their plantation labor, linked to the export economy. On occasion food might be produced by squads of slaves working together under a fore-man's direction; but that was not an effective or popular solution. There were also serious problems with importing food. When war or weather interrupted overseas imports the slaves, malnourished anyway and usually hungry, might literally starve to death.[11]

But there was a third way to obtain food and that was to enable the slaves to produce it themselves, on a family basis. This solution was first tried in Jamaica early in the eighteenth century or even ear-lier, and it turned out to be enormously successful. We can infer that by 1735, production of the bulk of slave subsistence by individ-ual slaves and their families had become island-wide, because by that date they were being allowed to sell fresh produce (except meat) anywhere on the island (Mintz 1975).[12]

The custom was to assign plots of plantation land unsuitable for sugarcane to individual slaves. Such plots were usually not fertile or well watered; they lay in gullies, or covered in brush, or far from the plantation center. No one supposed that the slaves came to own such land by virtue of working it, and of course they had no legal claim over it. Yet it became the practice to respect the slave's labor investment in land he worked for himself. If the planter wanted such a plot of land for a different purpose, it was expected everywhere in the island that he would make available to the slave cultivator land of equal quality and quantity to plant elsewhere and would pay for any lost product. A famous eighteenth-century Jamaican writer, Bryan Edwards, uses the old Latin term *peculium*—land held by a slave as private property—to refer to the slave's claim. The word continued to appear in descriptions of the slaves' customary, not le-gal, claim on resources in which their own labor had been invested.[13]

Though I have not found evidence that either planter or slave ever gave much public attention to the practice, its everyday reality meant that a basic aspect of the relationship between slaves and masters had been changed. Slaves accepted the opportunity to grow their own food. Though it increased their exploitation on the one hand by requiring even more of their labor, it made it possible for them to eat far better on the other. It also gave them a chance to mobilize family labor; and then to produce goods that they could take to market and sell; to use their brains to do sums, make choices, plan, and figure; and in these ways to take part autonomously in the wider Jamaican economy. Seen in the light of two centuries, these varied advantages may actually have been as important as the food itself—though the malnutrition imposed on people by the plantation is famous. We have difficulty imagining how, given the cruelty of plantation labor, the slaves would be able to judge the value of their uncoerced, personal individual effort. But the opportunity to produce their own food with the help of family and then to market it so that their independent planning, however modest, could be judged as part of their own achievements must have taken on tremendous meaning.

The planters benefited from the slaves' food-growing labor, which was wrung out of the little time they had left after working under the drivers in the plantation fields. But the slaves also benefited. Their basic benefit was nutritive. But more, perhaps, than we can measure, it mattered that this was their chance to exercise their own will. The plantation labor system, after all, was kept in place by the constant threat and frequent use of violence. Though the slaves were never reduced to automatons by that system, planter ideology rested on the idea that they were inherently incapable of making any independent decisions. We see planter ideology deviating here sharply from planter practice, and there must have been other such deviations. Such contradictions emerged because otherwise powerless people were able to exploit the promise of benefit to the power-holders—though for a price, naturally.[14]

Soon the Jamaican internal market system was dominated by the slaves (Mintz 1955). When I first looked at Jamaican plantation history, that fact was borne in powerfully on me. How could it have happened, I wondered, that these abused, underfed, and overworked people, many of them recent arrivals from a different world, became the subsistence mainstay of the Jamaican economy? It seemed fundamentally to challenge my image of how the plantation operated. But because the slaves learned in this manner to produce their own food, to go to market to buy and sell, to plan their own labor and that of their families, and even to accumulate wealth, I called such people "proto-peasants"—peasants yet still slaves; peasants-to-be; peasants "in embryo" (Mintz 1961).

The emergence of the slaves themselves as an economic force outside the plantations within slave-era Jamaica was one of the trade-offs negotiated with the planters. But over time it became a trade-off with which the planters learned to live. Such economic activity by the slaves—deemed incapable of even the simplest tasks without the blessings of white instruction, slavery rhetoric declared—made clear that the entire system rested not on any basic difference between slave and master in race, culture, intellect, religion, or anything else but ultimately on the whip, the branding iron, and endless amounts of hot air, angrily huffed and puffed in defense of forced labor, on the island and in Parliament.[15] I suppose that the slaves must have known this. They themselves were active participants in bargains they struck with the planters—poor bargains though they may have been in some ways. It bears noting that when we acknowledge negotiation as a practice between unequals, it does not make the unequals into equals or justify oppression. It simply allows us to understand better how they survive in each other's company. The slaves were legally defenseless, despite any economic gains they might make: "slaves were capitalists without the benefit of laws protecting property and person" (Burnard 2004:154–156, 252–254).

Between the end of the slave trade to the British West Indian colonies in 1808 and the official and public emancipation of the slaves in Jamaica on August 1, 1838, there were many turns in the road. Emancipation was to have come in 1834. But the act that ended slavery did not emancipate the slaves. They were instantly converted by law into forced laborers. This was called the Apprenticeship, a cruel institution designed to continue to exploit the slaves and to reward their masters (Holt 1992; Paton 2001, 2004). This terrible transitional interval was intended to last for at least six years, but it ended on August 1, 1838, when in Jamaica alone, more than 310,000 slaves became free.

It is not possible fully to capture the planter mindset. But as owners of a defenseless labor supply that had been exploited in every way and was held in great contempt, the masters were so corrupted by their power that they were apparently at first unable to deal at all with the very idea that the labor force was now free.

But of course the planters' need for labor, real and imagined, did not end. The momentous change in status—and it *was* momentous—was accompanied by a wide variety of acts by the planters aimed at limiting the power of the newly freed and at foredooming any attempt by freed persons to improve their economic and political status (Knox 1977; Mintz 1979).

Probably the most important change Emancipation brought to the Jamaican people, beyond the reality of emancipation itself, was the sharp decline in planters' access to labor and the parallel rise of peasant villages, many under religious leadership. Holt (1992) provides a thorough and convincing overview of the fate of the free people from the years just preceding the Apprenticeship almost to the mid-twentieth century. He shows that during the Apprenticeship the lot of the apprentices was very bitter, and though they were no longer slaves and received some protection from the stipendiary magistrates, or supplementary judges, who had been installed for their defense, they continued to suffer greatly.

When the labor available to the planters was sharply reduced with emancipation, they tried by various means to convince or coerce the free people to work just as they had before, now for low wages. Holt (1992:146–76) explains that freed people were opting for a basically different kind of economy than the one plantation labor represented and made possible. In their zeal to buy even tiny bits of land, the schooling they sought for their children, their cultivation of the land, and their marketing of its products, the newly free demonstrated their basic desire for economic independence. Many were willing to work some on the plantations (if not always on the terms the planters offered). But they wanted even more to be economically independent of them.

Between Emancipation and 1865, the struggle of the planter economy to secure labor—in the quantities and at the prices it claimed to need—continued. Legislative ruses were created by the

Jamaica Assembly both to subjugate the newly freed and to import cheap contract labor with which to undercut the bargaining power of the Jamaicans in the reordered labor market. But people did not submit quietly. The number of small farms owned by free people grew. The markets, full of the agricultural and craft products of these free peasants, did well. A few export commodities were also produced by the peasantry; their success was attested to with particular eloquence by the American William Sewell (1968). In 1861, claims that the newly free were unwilling to work or to produce more than they ate or were uninterested in exporting their products, or raising their standard of living, were exaggerated; many such claims were simply false.

But there clearly was a struggle, much of it concealed or masked, between the planter economy and that of the peasantry. Squatting on abandoned or ruinate agricultural estates increased. Holt shows how the struggle was reflected in island politics. In the Jamaica Assembly, both the intersection of race and class and the divisions among Assembly members resulted in some legislation that eventually caused growing embitterment among small holders. The pressure to hold back the political will of the peasantry turned "race" into a social difference as important as property. The few free colored legislators in the assembly, most of them owners of land themselves, were caught between the wealthy and powerful planters on the one hand, and the increasingly desperate, landless or land-starved, smallholders and squatters on the other. The planters aimed to immobilize the newly freed as a landless labor force. The colored, whom the poor thought of as their natural allies, felt obliged to protect their own stakes, even though they were keenly aware of the need for land among the rural poor.

The persisting, long-term objective of the plantation owners was to secure labor at prices acceptable to them. Their ability to control the situation worsened after 1846, however, when the duties on sugar were equalized and Jamaican sugar produced by free people had to compete with Cuban sugar produced by slaves. Moreover, the planters feared that a free black majority population, much of it apparently committed to a peasant way of life, would become a political threat to them and to the plantation system if it became enfranchised.

In 1865, the Morant Bay rising—Catherine Hall's (1992:208) appropriate term for what is usually called a rebellion—altered the picture catastrophically. Heuman (1994) has provided a detailed account of the events leading up to the Rebellion, and calls it that. Holt (1992) uncovers some of the causes of unrest, shows that the disorder was not wholly unpremeditated, and argues on good grounds that religion played a part in the leadership of the rebels. Rebellion or rising, the Morant Bay disturbance began as a land riot, and it resulted in multiple killings of white officials by a mob. It was brought about by various sources of unease and resentment, including the deafness of local government and the Colonial Office to the repeated pleas of the peasantry for access to more land. Holt and Heuman both describe the elite's persisting and nasty racism in regard to political action and the redress of abuses.

The repression that followed Morant Bay caused an international scandal. Martial law imposed by Governor Edward Eyre resulted in the violent deaths of hundreds and led to his recall. Aware of the peril of a political system that might allow poor free people to vote, local government abdicated its power in the Assembly, and the Crown restored to Jamaica the status of Crown colony, such that it would be ruled directly from Britain. While Morant Bay did not destroy the possibility of a successful evolution of a viable Jamaican peasant society, it did make its emergence far more difficult.[16] There simply was no political means for arguing that a free, prosperous peasantry and a plantation economy might coexist. After 1865 and the Jamaica Assembly's decision to abolish itself in favor of Crown rule, it was the freed people who were blamed for the breakdown of order. "Race" and "human nature" were to blame. The truth was that reluctance to permit the growth of a black political constituency had gone hand in hand with a desire to inhibit the growth of a prosperous small farmer class.

For the planters, the reversion to Crown rule was a better outcome than one in which the Jamaican people might achieve a political voice and economic power. Jamaica's history followed a course roughly like that of other British West Indian colonies. To be sure, each was unique; yet they shared some features.[17] In nearly all, economic power after emancipation was vested in a small white ruling group. Similarly, each social structure had at least three tiers, usually consisting of white planters, a tiny mixed-race middle class, and a larger number of poor (mostly landless) black freed persons. In all, one's physical appearance was an index and, to some degree, a determinant of social status and life chances. Jamaica was the most populous and important British Caribbean colony when freedom came. Jamaica—more than 350 years since becoming a British colony, and now long independent—still retains, I believe, noticeable threads of continuity with its colonial past.

When slavery ended in Jamaica in 1834, the missionary churches, backed by the abolitionists with the United Kingdom got much of the credit. Large numbers of slaves had joined the Methodist, Baptist, and other missionary churches. They and their ministers found that planter intemperance—which, before Emancipation, included the burning of churches (Mathieson 1926)—ultimately provided them with more sympathetic supporters and listeners in Britain. The planters in the British West Indies were treated gingerly by the Colonial Office. Freedom for the slaves was viewed as the loss of their costly human property, even though everything would be done to secure their access to the labor of the slaves after they became free. Jamaican planters were given a large part of the advance compensation approved by Parliament (the total of which came to £20,000,000);[18] and more time in which to exploit their slaves, now redefined (1834–38) as "apprentices."[19] Of course nothing was done by the Colonial Office to ease the transition for the slaves—only for the planters. The Jamaica Assembly did all it could to keep the ex-slaves as powerless as before. They had been providing cheap labor (and much else) for their masters for centuries; they presumably would do the same once they were free. It was expected—and surely it was hoped—that freedom would not interfere with the continued subjection of people, though now legally free, to the plantation system.[20]

When I went to Jamaica to begin summer fieldwork in June 1952, I knew what I wanted to study. Upon the early termination of Apprenticeship in 1838, the idea arose among the missionaries to create agricultural villages on which to settle freed people by buying up failed estates, where land was exhausted (or as local usage had it, "ruinate"), hence relatively cheap.[21] These would be divided into small plots to be resold to the parishioners. The free village movement was the creature of the missionary churches, whose leaders had provided encouragement for the laws that led eventually to Emancipation and who could envision such free villages as religious communities. The missionaries had come around only slowly to a position openly opposed to slavery. It would be naive to imagine that their conception of the possible future for the freed would take serious account of what had been the slaves' own deep desires. More understandably, the missionaries' motives for backing the free village system fitted with their ideas of how best to supervise and maintain the religious life of the newly freed.

The village movement they created was not intended to attack planter power, but it was threatening to the planters and was perceived that way. It offered at least a partial economic alternative to wage labor and a social alternative to living as freed persons on (and subject to) the plantations. The free village idea contained a vision of life after slavery that perhaps no one, except possibly the slaves, may have imagined. The movement envisioning villages composed of freed persons became central to the development of postslavery Jamaica. What the missionaries were doing (though I think not what they primarily intended to do) was making it possible to imagine the growth of a sturdy rural landowning class. But what the planters wanted, if they could no longer have slaves, was a rural proletarian sector—wage earners, but politically as defenseless as the slaves had been.

The planters understood that the most effective way to prevent "labor problems" would be to keep the newly freed landless. They knew that cheap labor would be most easily obtainable if there were more needy people than jobs; and they keenly resented having to pay anything at all for their labor.[22] Despite the indemnities that had been paid them for the loss of their human property, the planters bitterly hated the *fact* of emancipation. Many felt that the freed people were ingrates for wanting to be free and even more for wanting to move away from the plantations. The planters begrudged them the shacks they occupied on plantation land and passed ejectment laws under which to charge them rent or drive them from those shacks. The planters supposed that because their ancestors were often buried on the plantations and because friends lived nearby, the newly freed would be reluctant to leave, even if they were maltreated. They were right; but not entirely.

Apprenticeship had brought with it the stipendiary magistrates who were to adjudicate between masters and apprentices. On occasion the apprentices were found justified in their complaints, but often they were punished instead. Many—not all—of the magistrates sided repeatedly with the planters; most associated primarily with the planters (Marshall 1977; Paton 2001). The early end of Apprenticeship was clearly linked to the airing of its abuses in the United Kingdom.

Once freedom came, the planters in the Assembly tried to import additional labor, indentured labor, from India and China so as to increase the available supply and drive down its price. Their immigration schemes were financed by such means as leveling taxes on shingles imported for building workers' houses and on peasants' food needs such as imported flour and salt cod (Mintz 1979).

To a large extent, the newly freed appeared to be willing to work for the planters even for derisory wages. But access to land they could use to produce their own food—the very practice they had learned as proto-peasants—would keep their families fed while improving their bargaining position. In their view, anything that made land available that they could cultivate was good. At the same time and for the same reasons, the chance to move off the plantations would be to their advantage. And so the "free village system" was a genuine threat in the eyes of the planters. Because it could become a step toward landowning and economic security for the freed, the planters' perception of it was accurate.

In just one decade, the number of free villages multiplied (Mintz 1958a, 1974). Rev. John Clark, the Baptist minister who founded Sturge Town, the village in which I worked, reported in 1852 that about three-fourths of the enfranchised people in his district were settled in twenty different free villages (Clark 1852). The movement eventually may have affected as many as 100,000 persons—about one-third of those freed in 1838. Free people produced more than their own food; they produced and marketed food for the whole island. They also undertook to export modest quantities of exports that could be grown and processed on small farms, such as pimento (allspice), ginger, and goatskins (Sewell 1968). They were moving toward greater economic independence by working land, both rented and owned and used for both subsistence and production for overseas markets. These gains were accompanied by greater political assertiveness. Exports of sugar, rum, and molasses fell sharply, but the internal market system grew (Mintz and Hall 1960), as did the peasant class. By the time of the events at Morant Bay three decades later, however, availability of land for peasant farming had declined. The owners of estates, fully represented in the Assembly, saw the achievements of the peasantry as intolerable challenges to the plantation system. The planters' premise—that the labor available should exceed the number of workers actually needed—harmonized with their belief that any agricultural production not controlled by the plantations was a threat.

But virtue rarely reposes only on one side of an issue. The missionaries wanted to found free villages. They had in mind one-church villages settled by pious and obedient parishioners. After 1838, Jamaican peasants were expected to be faithful to the particular church that had saved them and to practice their worship as they had been instructed, in an unemotional Christian manner. There was condescension as well as severity in the missionary outlook,[23] in spite of the generosity and courage missionaries had shown during slavery and Apprenticeship.

What I wanted to look at in my initial fieldwork in Jamaica was the growth of those church-created villages and what they came to mean to people. I thought that the economic and ideological basis underlying the creation of such communities would make them more like each other, and less like other rural communities in Jamaica and that those differences might have long-term sociological consequences for the people living in them. What I learned came later to seem to me like a confirmation of my expectations (Carnegie 1987; Mintz, 1958a).

On my first trip to Jamaica, I visited the village I'd learned most about by reading: Sturge Town in St. Ann Parish, named after the famed Quaker abolitionist Joseph Sturge. The apprentice James Williams (Paton 2001), whose remarkable narrative Joseph Sturge publicized so astutely to hasten the coming of emancipation, came from Penshurst, a pimento and cattle "pen," or farm.[24] Next to Penshurst was Knapdale, another pimento and cattle pen, and they both abutted on Angwin Crawl, the property that became Sturge Town in 1839.

Tom and Leah Belnavis and daughters,
Sturge Town, Jamaica, 1952.

Reverend John Bee, the Baptist minister in Brown's Town in 1952, kindly helped me visit the village. After two days of meeting with people there, listening to them, and looking around, I decided to live there for the summer. It was too little time to do much, but it was all the time I had. Among the people I met in Sturge Town were Tom Belnavis, his wife Leah, their daughters Catherine and Thelma, and their neighbors. Tom Belnavis was a land-poor peasant. He was at first rather shy; I came to know him only slowly. He was not a member of the local Baptist church, not even a churchgoer. But he did like to sing at services, and at times would go to them to sing; he was known and admired for his voice. His wife and daughters attended the Tabernacle Church, a group that had broken off from the original Baptist church in Sturge Town in the 1850s.

Local people plainly liked Tom. They called him brother *(brud-dah)*; but they did not consider him a successful person, and indeed he was financially very hard pressed. I learned about that, listening to him:

> I have two quarters of land down in the bottom there around the house, and two acres in Bamboo (a couple of miles away). I got one quarter from a man died down there and I bought it. Another quarter my grandfather left me here when he died. I was one of five children, all boys. I was the oldest, the only bastard. My mother married another after she get me, and my brothers dem really half-brothers. I was raised here in my grandfather's house; he was from here. My great-grandmother, she came here to live. She was born as the slavery ended; she was get the night they make freedom. She was born nine months after. My grand-father raise me here. His father owned the land where the

church stands now. I went to school when the school there, back of the church—you can see the foundation. I went only till I was eleven. The teacher strict, and I didn't take to the school. Two years of that I spent there under that cabbage leaf tree, hiding from the school. When I was eleven, I start man work, working for myself. I have twenty-eight years on the road work; when the headman comes he must learn from me. You passed the bottom of the big hill on your way to Penshurst today—you mark the marl there? I put that in—they pay three shillings per chain, and I put in near to three days there. One day; then second day my pick broke; third day, yesterday, I finished. Hard work, man; but I like hard work. If I don't work hard, I can't sleep. Last year I worked on Llandovery Estate, sugar work. I worked night shift, came home at six o'clock in the morning, and [when I arrived] I left for my field with my pick and my hoe in my hand. I paid thirty-four shillings to get my land cleared and readied, and I put in 1,240 heads of cocos [taro]; but if a man didn't give me some cocos last week, I wouldn't taste them this year. The land is not right for cocos—weak it is. It is good to the corn, but I forced it with the cocos. The land need the rest; if you can't turn it to rest, it weaken. Look down there in the bottom, some have an acre and some a half, some only a quarter, or none at all. The land heavy with everything all in one place—coco, yam, breadfruit tree, they grow atop one another. We need land, man. The estates they won't rent. Mr. Cox at Knapdale [estate] say he's afraid of fire. [Tom laughs.] (field notes, July 9, 1952:26–27)

Tom Belnavis had much more to say. But for where he figures in my story, this is nearly enough. He was a Jamaican peasant, and in

many ways like most Caribbean peasants. But mentioning Tom requires me to say more about how the community in which he and
his family lived was organized. I'd come to Sturge Town because of
its historic place in the evolution of the so-called free villages. I will
make no serious attempt here to describe the social hierarchy of
Sturge Town. But any visitor there would have noticed differences
in the size of houses, the condition of their exteriors, and other
signs of material wealth: water catchments, electric wiring, stone
paths. Though people dressed quite alike and very simply for each
work day, when they wore their Sunday best, one saw many more
differences among them. Which church (if any) a person attended
was an index of social position, and of course the church officers
were special. Harder to learn but even more telling was whether a
person owned land and, if so, how much. If he needed help to work
his land; if he made any land available for others to work; if he ever
hired a truck to carry out produce—all those differences were part
of his standing. I became aware of these differences, and made a
good start at finding out how much land each local person had. But
it was far too big an enterprise for a single summer. When the time
came to go home, I was left with my field notes, whatever else I'd
scraped together and written down, and some ideas about what I
had found out.

Among the first Sturge Town people I met, even before Tom Belnavis, were two brothers. One lived in Sturge Town; the other had
moved to a newly built house nearby in the Knapdale settlement,
where he owned land. Marcus and Headley Williams were relatively
wealthy (for a village like Sturge Town)—faithful churchgoers who
attended the founding church of the village. One was a church dea-
con; both were church officers. Unlike Tom, they both owned a lot

A typical peasant house, Sturge Town, Jamaica.

of land—though I never found out exactly how much. Many of their habits and attitudes were different from Tom's—but not all.

Perhaps the first thing I learned in Sturge Town, without being told, was that every male who lived there worked worked the land. There were exceptions, but very few. Marcus and Headley were among those who thought of farming as life itself rather than primarily as work. Though they dressed in proper black suits for Sunday services, I don't know if I ever saw either in shoes or long pants otherwise. I remember them best in shorts and loose shirts, going to their fields or coming from them. They were then men in their late thirties, perhaps: robust, black, handsome, industrious and sociable. Good friends—serious, interesting, conservative in outlook, in their behavior both traditional and parsimonious, embodying what Eric Wolf once referred to in his work on peasants as "the cult of poverty." Here is what I mean.

My meals were brought to me at regular times, from Mrs. Stern's house down the road, and cooked for me by Bob Henry's wife. One time I was sitting in the little house next to the church that I'd been given to use, and Marcus Williams was with me when I was brought my dinner. We were talking when my food arrived. I asked Marcus if he had eaten, and he said yes, he had. So I started to eat. I finished eating. I'd had—I think it was—ackee and salt fish, with rice and peas, but it was more than I could eat. And I said, "Well I've eaten just about all I can." And I noticed that Marcus was looking at my plate, rather the way a cat looks at a bird. And it occurred to me—I mean, I'd been eating—I said "Marcus, are you sure you wouldn't like some?" And then he said "I would not refuse," and he picked up my fork and plate and finished the food. I don't think he was all that hungry; he had refused when I'd first offered him some. But he also

Gully cultivation, Sturge Town, Jamaica.

was not going to let good food just sit there like that. I thought this was a demonstration of Marcus' outlook or philosophy, and I felt better, seeing the food eaten and the plate empty. Not surprisingly, it was also the way I was raised.

Headley would talk about being up in New Jersey as a migrant laborer—and this is now more than half a century ago. The Jamaicans there would want to go to church on Sunday, and had to walk much of the way, and they carried their little valises on their heads. Headley took pleasure in recounting how they would walk single file along the highway, valises on their heads, and how the passing cars would slow down so people could ogle them—these black men walking single file with things on their heads, as if they were in Africa. Both Marcus and Headley went to the United States to work. Jamaicans, including country people, have been migrating to work in other countries since the end of the Apprenticeship. It was a means for sustaining those they left behind, but equally important, it was always a way of saving money to buy land.

Land came up over and over and over again. I asked Headley one day about exchange labor ("day fe day")—the practice of labor exchange among cultivators, a group of whom works one man's fields one day and another's the next day. Day fe day was traditionally accompanied by a midday meal, supplied by the ground master (host). There would be music; and Headley explained to me that the musician was called the burner because his music made the time pass faster. If they were planting or hoeing, and one man fell back, those on either side of him would move faster, then plant or hoe the row for the laggard in order to shame him. When I asked Headley why day fe day was dying out, he explained that men differ in their willingness to work as hard on another man's field as on their own.

So there comes the reluctance to treat every man's labor as equal, because the hardest working participants get cheated.

The feelings about land and labor in Sturge Town were strong and clearly expressed the individualism of Jamaican peasants. There is an odd conundrum here. Caribbean peasants acquired their individualism in the era of slavery, during their creolization. It was consistent, I think, with the values and attitudes of the Europeans. Yet the peasants of Jamaica were clearly thought by the whites to have failed to become like the Europeans. In the eyes of many, they were perceived to have failed as free people. Holt (1992), among others, has pointed this out. Commenting on Holt's study and speaking of slavery in several New World countries, Lichtenstein notes that Holt "recognize[s] that the freed people made their way in a bourgeois world that equated morality with personal ambition and self-discipline in the marketplace, and weighted success on the scales of individual acquisitiveness. The apparent failure of many if not most freed people to make the grade by these standards did much to reconfirm the racial presumptions of southern planters, former abolitionists, and carpetbagger capitalists alike" (1998:128).

Caribbean peasants were (and those who remain are) quite unlike other peasants elsewhere—European or Asian peasants, or even Latin American peasants, in places like Germany or Burma or Ecuador. They are often people of largely African origin whose ancestors were kept in slavery, some over the course of centuries.[25] Their forebears had mostly first learned to be peasants while still enslaved, as proto-peasants, and then became peasants. Said differently, Caribbean rural cultivators are "reconstituted" peasants (Mintz 1961). After slavery they had eked out their livings by making a little cash working on the road, or in sugar fields or mills, or raising pigs or goats or chickens for market. A few raised cows. They made buttons, combs, and drum heads from the bones, horns, and skins of their animals. They collected withes and made baskets and winnowing trays and fish traps from them, fashioned plates and bowls and spoons from local wood, carved gourds into bowls and canteens, grew essential oil plants, rendered beeswax and honey, functioned as healers, traded their labor, and healed, castrated and butchered their animals. Like peasants everywhere, such people had to have some access to cash, because they could not produce everything they consumed, such as clothing, shoes, metal tools, or their children's school notebooks. They might barter or trade work for some of what they needed; but they could not do so for all of it. Government always demanded something from them, in labor or products or, ever more commonly, in cash. Like nearly all peasants through history, they were hardly ever able to live adequately by using only the resources that they owned or had access to, so in one way or another they had to sell some of their labor—often that of their children (Wolf 1956:206–208).[26]

Most of them are poor (not all); but all of them, including the richest in most places, have lived feeling under attack for centuries. This is not paranoia. It seems to me that being a Caribbean peasant came to mean feeling attacked all of the time simply because one *was* under attack all of the time. Caribbean roads have never been constructed with peasants in mind; and agronomic services have only rarely been made available with peasants in mind.

Though there have been hundreds of thousands—perhaps millions—of reconstituted peasants in the Caribbean region during these last three centuries, none has left us any eloquent testimonial to their aspirations, experiences, or values. But when we look at the places where Caribbean peasantries did form, it is clear that making a secure living on the land, being able to produce farm commodities for sale, and passing on their way of life and adequate resources to their children were probably always among the basic objectives of such people (Wolf 1966).

Educating peasants to citizenship was almost the last service that any Caribbean government, colonial or not, ever thought of providing them. Tom Belnavis had never been taught that societies need infrastructures, public education, courts, governments, police, professional schools. Most of the time Caribbean peasantries did not have such things on their minds, except as they faced their own desperate needs in daily life. They have always been too busy struggling for a secure economic base. In most places, the struggle was against forces aimed mostly at pushing them off their own land and back onto the plantations; or these days, into cities to wash dishes or make beds, or overseas. Yet Tom Belnavis knew that schools are a crucial route for the advancement of one's children in democratic societies. He also knew governments must have means to sustain their roads and hospitals. I knew from what he told me that he was willing to see his own tiny cash income taxed if it would support any of his basic needs, especially schools and medical care.

I am convinced after my Caribbean experiences that what people like Tom or Marcus and Headley aspired to during the last century or two was never considered a realistic societal goal, either by the colonial government or by the governments that have succeeded it. In Jamaica, as elsewhere in the region, the equivalent of the black North American dream of forty acres and a mule died hard. But everywhere that it bloomed it was killed off, more by intent than by neglect, or perhaps by a mix of both. Those who thought about

land the way Tom Belnavis did were not easy to kill off. But in this
last half century, the chance to escape poverty by mass emigration
and the generalized oppression of a poor, still-colonial society in
which the rewards for industry, honesty, and integrity are few have
led over time to the near death of the Jamaican peasantry, indeed of
Caribbean peasantry nearly everywhere.[27]

In Jamaica, that peasantry lives—or at least, lived—in the shadow
of the national history. In between the slaves and the masters grew
the social grouping I referred to earlier, separated from the other
two by color, social status, economic niche, and political and cultural values. Over time that middle group became Jamaica's middle
class, both rural and urban. But much of what divided them from
the slaves continued to divide them from freed people and their descendants ever after; and these historical "residues" figure in my
story. In what follows, two threads of social history in the life of the
local people stand out in particular. One has to do with race—what
it is, how people perceive such differences, its persisting presence in
the awareness and attitudes of individuals. Another is gender—how
men and women think they differ from each other and turn their
thoughts into social realities that sometimes end up perpetuating
how they think.

Back in 1952, I would accompany Sturge Town's higglers, or market women, to market. Brown's Town marketplace was about seven
miles' walk from Sturge Town, mostly over hard-rock paths that followed the boundary between the large estates that encircled Sturge
Town. It was my habit to walk to town with the Sturge Town higglers on Friday at dusk and stay there to take notes on the buying
and selling until late the following morning. It was my first relatively lengthy contact with women marketers, and I fell in love with

their keen eye for a razor's edge of profit, their vigor and daring. Walking to town carrying a notebook, while they trotted happily along with forty pounds' worth or more of fresh produce on their heads, was both a joy—and humbling.

Not far from where the path to Sturge Town joined the larger path to Brown's Town, there was a fork in the road. It led to a nearby cattle pen, owned by a prosperous local pen keeper, who was a man of light color. I had never met him, but I had been told who he was. He figures in my story.

On one occasion after I'd slept overnight in the market and was preparing to hike back to Sturge Town, I stopped by the small store and filling station of a friend of mine in town to say hello. I found my friend Pat, himself a light-complexioned man, quite upset. It turned out that very early that morning, the owner of the pen near Sturge Town had shot a man out of a tree on his farm. He had said it happened because the man whom he shot was trespassing, stealing mangoes. He denied having meant to shoot him; in fact, he claimed he'd simply discharged his shotgun over his head, without realizing the man was in the tree. A likely story, as we say. In any case the trespasser was wounded, and Pat said many people were upset. Pat himself was disturbed, angry about an act he called "stupid and dangerous." We talked briefly. I was preparing to leave him to start my walk back—my higgler friends would not be leaving for home for a while—when suddenly who should drive up in his pickup truck but the self-same pen-keeper.

He was about Pat's color—by which I mean that he probably would not have been seen as other than white in the U.S. North. In the U.S. South, some people would notice that he was—as North Americans used to say—"colored," whether or not they said so.[28] I listened to Pat asking him questions. Then Pat introduced me. The man said: "So you've been living in Sturge Town?" I explained my work. "I'm on my way home now," he said; "I can drop you at the fork. But I'd like to give you lunch." I agreed to come; I wanted to find out more if I could about a man like him, who would use a shotgun on a mango thief. When we reached his house—it turned out to be a very large, comfortable farmhouse in the Jamaican style—he made me a drink and left me in the library awaiting lunch. I looked at the books there and came upon a school notebook, with what I took to be the name of the pen-keeper's daughter inside the cover. Though it was ostensibly for taking notes and there were mostly school notes in it, it also contained sketches or caricatures of the nastiest racist kind. They were labeled to show that they were of the artist's schoolteachers. I had never seen such cruel depictions by—I supposed—a child before, and was shocked by the terrible, unfeeling venom they betrayed on the part of the artist. I was also caught up in North American perceptions—it occurred to me that the artist was not "all white" herself—recognizing, with another shock, my own North American brand of racism.[29]

My host called out to me, and I joined him in the dining room, hastily returning the notebook to its place. Lunch was served. I was still somewhat bemused by my host's sudden friendliness; he, his wife, and I lunched nearly in silence. Then, during the dessert, there was a knock at the door, and when the maid went to admit the visitors, it turned out to be the constables from Brown's Town, who had come to bring my host to town. Suddenly I understood why I was so welcome. My host was happy to have a foreigner—a scholar and a *buckra* (white person)—at his table when the police came for him.

The following week when I returned to Brown's Town market, I learned that the night following the pen keeper's arraignment, someone had cut the udders off half a dozen of his cows—vengeance for his insouciance with a shotgun. The hostility of the poor and mostly black toward the relatively well-off conformed neatly to the differences in "race" between the poor and the well-off. It was, it seemed to me at the time, an enduring hostility, with ancient roots.

And yet I was not surprised, all the same, to discover that many of the villagers among whom I was living, including Tom and Headley, thought that the trigger-happy dairyman was justified. They did not like his shooting the thief. But they thought that stealing food was particularly hateful. "Praedial" theft—stealing agricultural produce—is a curse among farmers everywhere, and one of the commonest and most demoralizing problems of Caribbean peasant life.[30]

Though race was not much talked about in Sturge Town, it did come up frequently in conversation—sometimes in reference to slavery, other times in reference to wealth. An old lady who was my neighbor in Sturge Town had once worked for an estate owner elsewhere. He was a direct descendant of Peter Blagrove, one of the regicides whom Cromwell had rewarded with a huge land grant in western Jamaica in the late 1650s, after the island fell to the British. This lady was recounting to us her excitement long ago when she was obliged to oversee preparations for the wedding feast of her employer's son. When she looked out of the kitchen, she said, and saw the "hundred *buckra*" waiting for the meal, she was terrified. Tom Belnavis snorted with laughter. "'Buckra,' we call dem; and all o' dem mulatta."

My friend Tom Belnavis, Headley and Marcus, and the pen-keeper are figures from a tableau composed of the people of Sturge Town and its environs. Though surely they never thought of it that way, to outsiders like myself they represented the people of Jamaica, and of that parish. Getting to know them, one entered into the fabric of social relations in a new place and learned how people inside it treated its daily demands, obligations, and rewards as life itself—which, for them, it is. Recording one day's events in June, 1952, I wrote in my field diary:

> Tom talks about how working hard enables him to sleep. But his wife, Miz' Leah, works hard, too, and on the road as well. He breaks up marl with his pick; she kneels, hammer in hand, on a burlap rag made from a sugar bag and breaks the marl down into small pieces so that it becomes roadbed before my eyes. She moves forward a few inches at a time. After greeting her, I kneel beside her, and she allows me to break some marl with her hammer, to see that—like nearly everything one learns to do in fieldwork, it seems to me—it is not as easy as it looks. Miz' Leah is lighter-skinned than Tom; her family didn't want her to marry him, he tells me. And so, he says, he made her pregnant first, and then her family consented.

It was easy to see what made Tom attractive. He had a big voice and sang well; people liked his expansive, cocky manner. He was a rebel of a kind in a community famed in the parish for the obedience and respectability of its inhabitants. That reputation for compliant comportment probably came from Sturge Town's start as a Baptist village. People in St. Ann would say that if you wanted a good serving girl you should get one from Sturge Town. But Sturge Town was encircled by large estates, such that it was hard to rent any land to cultivate, and impossible to buy any.[31] Though the "free villages" differed from each other, partly because of where they were, they had a history that began with free people moving onto land of their own, among people like themselves, practicing the same religion and believing in the same particular deity. I suppose that within a single generation nearly all of those villages were suffering for want of land. Sturge Town, hemmed in on all sides by large estates, felt that land hunger acutely.

Tom's shoes were rough over-the-ankle boots made in Jamaica by country cobblers. He nailed horse shoes to their soles to keep them from wearing out. People knew that when "Bruddah" came down the road singing, sparks sometimes flew from his shoes. Tom was acutely aware that Sturge Town was full of well-behaved people, people with more property and more airs than he. It annoyed him that he could not get his hands on more land there; the church had some to rent, but of course it favored the regular churchgoers. Miz' Leah helped him make a go of things with her work on the road. She saved for the girls' education. Tom said women have better heads for business than men—a view shared by a surprisingly large number of Jamaican males.

Tom's vocation as a peasant clung to him. After one of my trips to town with the higglers, I stopped by the Chinese grocery in Brown's Town—at that time nearly every town in Jamaica had a Chinese grocery—to buy a present for him. In the refrigerated food case, I found an apple—an imported rarity in Jamaica, and one I was sure he had never tasted. He was touched by my gift, and we ate it together. But he was extremely careful when he cut it open—

because he wanted the seeds. "I need to see if I can make the seeds dem grow," he said reflectively. They did, but only briefly. His interest in growing things differed somewhat, I thought—though not entirely—from that of a skilled American backyard vegetable grower. For Tom, the land, the soil, *meant* something different. It did not yield to him, but he seemed to love it.

Jamaica was a society in which new or added class distinctions developed slowly. For most of its history, it has been a kind of colonial squirearchy—but the squires were sugar planters. Between them and the slaves—and I use the preposition "between" somewhat uneasily—there were the free colored people, whose allegiances were by no means uniform, and who changed their stands, sometimes unexpectedly (Holt 1992). Not until the mid-nineteenth century, with the end of protectionism for West Indian sugar and the growing pressure on land-hungry free people, did that hardened, yet weakened, structure begin to give way. Since slavery had ended only in 1834–1838 and the Morant Bay Rebellion had led to the return of Crown rule after 1865, planter power had endured, even though less and less bound solely to the land.

Throughout the last century, people like Tom Belnavis clung to the bits of land they had or tried to get some land of their own. There was the long-established and important practice I have already mentioned of emigrating to make money and coming back to buy land with it; or adding to the bit one had by buying yet another small piece next to it. Some of the land would be family land, a specific term for land that was neither to be divided nor sold and to which kinship was the only mode of access, as Jean Besson's fine work has made clear (Besson 2002). But family land alone was not enough to preserve the peasantry, economically and politically.

Tom's and Leah's ancestors came to freedom with a healthy respect for gender equality, particularly when they acquired land. Jamaican slaves—the "proto-peasants"—had been taking their produce to market for more than a century before freedom came. The accounts of the eighteenth century tell us that before freedom, whole families went the market place. After freedom (with certain important exceptions), internal marketing became largely a female specialization, while cultivation became mostly the work of males. Women are housekeepers and cooks; but they also do most of the "higglering" or marketing; they probably learn more about the market, about bargaining, about currency, than men. There was a widely shared opinion—perhaps only among poor rural Jamaicans, but I don't think so—that the claims spouses have on each other's wealth are different. Tom Belnavis thought so. So did other men in that village, though they revealed their feelings mostly in little harangues. One told me:

> If they have money you mus' beg dem for it, unless they are good and let you have it. But if you have money they have rights to all of it. It isn't fair. If you have a bad woman, perhaps she give your money to another man. But if she a good wife, it is just as well if she keeps it. I give mine all I have. I keep nothin', only small money for what I need. If you keep out something one time and she knows, then she always think you have more, and she demand it even when you not even got it. If you give her all, then she is responsible. (Field notes, May 31, 1952:62)

Men are more occupied with the crops than with the market. In a general way, males and females tend to divide up by occupation.

Men make furniture, baskets, do tailoring, cobble shoes, some iron-work; they do the fishing. Women make clothing, launder, shop for things to resell, sell baked goods, go to market, and may buy things there for resale in their villages.[32]

The readiness of Jamaican rural males to attribute superior commercial talent and knowhow to their wives, sisters, and daughters may spring from a real historical and gender difference in their relationship to the market. But because land is scarce and wage labor a nearly unavoidable source of additional income, men cannot farm with the same assurance that their wives can higgle. Though a class of moderately prosperous farmers exists, it is small; it grows slowly. The items that can be produced for export are limited; and the small-scale producers can look to the state for little or no help. The state has devoted itself to the needs of the plantations, the cattle farms, and (more recently) the dairies—not to those of the small-scale exporters. Men's work and women's work remain divided and complementary.

Race raises different issues. Jamaican rural people are sharply aware of differences in hair form, skin color, and so on. They have—as do Caribbean people everywhere—a complex glossary of description, as well as a rich reservoir of stories, jokes, and personal experiences, linked to race. A rural judge recounted to me his humiliation in the United States. He had gone to Miami for a minor operation, and was advised to stay at a nearby hotel. The next day as he crossed the lobby he heard someone calling out to him "Judge! Judge!" "I turned around," he said indignantly, "and there calling me, *and staying in the same hotel,* was a man who had once worked as my yard boy!" There are a hundred other tales—if not a thousand—that could be added to this one. The old North American primacy of race over class once came as a shock to foreign people of color, no matter how much they had heard about it.

North Americans visiting Jamaica (or Haiti) for the first time are likely to be struck by how dark people are in comparison to black Americans. There are not many who look like, say, Colin Powell, relative to the whole population. The social and economic scale corresponds quite faithfully to the scale of appearance, with the lighter people of course mostly near the top.

Tom saw the links between color and privilege, though he seemed more amused than bitter about them. I once asked him, after we had met at a church social event a man in a neighboring village who was nearly white, what Jamaicans thought when they met a poor white man. "A poor white man?" he repeated, smiling. "We laugh!"

When I first went to Jamaica, one could not find a salesgirl in the larger and more expensive stores in Kingston whose complexion was not light. I had no doubt that this was a coefficient of the way Jamaican racism worked. There were few professional jobs, and sales positions in the "best" stores were quite desirable. But I remembered that W. E. B. Du Bois had been warmly approving of Kingston's nearly white shopgirls, who, he wrote, with "a curl or tint . . . proclaimed the most ancient of blood" (Lewis 1993:456). And in 1948, when I met Dr. Eric Williams at a meeting in Puerto Rico, the same subject came up. Williams was bothered by the visible racism in Jamaica's best stores; but he was also impressed by the relaxed tenor of everyday race relations in Puerto Rico. He knew, of course, that both those societies were racist; but they differed in the form of its expression. And the perceptions of these two scholars clearly differed as well. While Du Bois had been pleased to see that none of those Jamaican shopgirls was entirely white, Williams was disappointed that none of them was very black.

The guesthouses in which I stayed during my first visits to Kingston were invariably operated by light-skinned women, usually unmarried; and I was given a concise reason why. "Their brothers marry English women while they're studying in the U.K., and bring them back. But since the sisters cannot marry beneath their color, they usually stay single," I was told. Haitians and Puerto Ricans would surely understand this; but its formulation would not mean precisely the same thing to them. I believe that neither in Haiti nor in Puerto Rico would such a marriage—between a lighter woman and a darker man, even in the middle class—be so harshly enjoined by society. Yet Haitians and Puerto Ricans would surely have agreed on the social significance of such a marriage.

Jamaica was not, is not, simply another example of a single species but a society in its own right, shaped in particular detail by its history, by the peoples who came to live in it, and by the imperial rule and the cultural forces to which it was subjected. The thirst for land that marked the end of slavery arose there as it did in the other cases to follow; the concern with color, with race, is as lively in Haiti or Puerto Rico as in Jamaica. But these three societies are truly different from each other, in ways best understood by listening to and watching the people who compose them. Conceding all of the risks this entails, at least the generalities with which one tries to make sense of things are constructed from what one sees of the lives, and hears from mouths, of the people who are right there living in their own way.

3

Haiti

THE SECOND of the ancient colonies is the "Black Republic"—the Western Hemisphere's second sovereign state, the Republic of Haiti.[1] A thinly settled Spanish colonial backwater until it became war booty, the western third of Santo Domingo was officially ceded to France in 1697. Long before, western Santo Domingo, nearly uninhabited, had become an international refuge area. Since Spain lacked adequate manpower to police effectively its own vast possessions in the New World, the region attracted army and navy deserters, vagabonds, and escaped criminals, occupiers of an "internal frontier" of the sort I described earlier. It became home to hunters who learned to live off the semiferal cattle that had been deliberately left there by the first Spaniards. Hunting down these animals with long lances to hamstring them, they smoked meat, made leather, and rendered tallow, all products they could trade to passing ships. These were the *boucaniers* ("meat smokers")—who would be reborn as the buccaneers of historical romances. Some became pirates and eventually respectable government figures, as in the case of Sir Henry Morgan.

Western Santo Domingo's pre-1697 history has been much romanticized. The people there were mostly French in origin—the

French actually installed a governor long before the cession by Spain. Yet this early frontier, much described, is really not well known. After 1697, however, as French Saint Domingue, it was rapidly transformed into the single most profitable colony in the history of the New World.[2] Most of the profit came from sugar, preceded by indigo and cotton and followed by coffee and other estate products. The new colony thrived; its products kept a huge French fleet busy. French capital, fertile land, and stolen labor—people stolen from Africa, labor from the captives themselves—yielded huge profits to the metropolis. Less than a hundred years later, that immensely profitable colony would become the setting for the biggest (and even more disturbing to the global status quo, most successful) slave revolt in world history. It ended with the former slaves in power, a hated but enduring thorn in the side of hemispheric slavery.

When Napoleon sent General Charles Victor-Emmanuel Leclerc, his brother-in-law, to the war-torn French colony in early 1802 to put down the Revolution there with the hope of eventually reenslaving the people, he told him to ship to France all of the leaders of the blacks, those "gilded Africans" who had become local heroes and might lead the freed slaves against the French if an attempt were made to restore slavery.[3] Most of all he had in mind General (hence "gilded") Toussaint Bréda, known as Louverture. Louverture had been the slave and coachman of a French planter on the Bréda Plantation at Haut-du-Cap, in the north of the colony. His owner had freed him, and over time he had become a renter of land and a coffee grower.

Louverture first came into view when the colony was under attack by Spain and then Great Britain, enemies of revolutionary

France, eager to seize its most lucrative tropical possession. Louverture took up arms on the side of an invading Spanish army. But then he switched to the French side (Geggus 2002), this time fighting against the English and the Spaniards—and rising to the rank of brigadier. Observers, biographers, even novelists have deemed Toussaint a strangely aloof figure, mercurial and contradictory. Some of his most critical decisions, made at political turning points, seem abrupt and unexpected. He was admired for his courage and tactical brilliance but known also for his silence—perhaps better said, secretiveness.[4] In 1800, Louverture was viewed as the preeminent military leader in Saint Domingue. Though considered by Napoleon a talented opportunist as well, he had appeared to be faithful to revolutionary France, ever since emancipation was officially declared by the National Convention in Paris in 1794. From then on, Louverture believed that the only guarantee of this new freedom would be the continuing economic success of the plantations. He was convinced that if the plantation economy collapsed, the French armies would soon be back to restore slavery. He dedicated himself fiercely to keep the plantations in operation, and developed a labor code for the management of the newly freed, imposing it on people in the regions he held militarily, and using it with considerable success to keep the plantations working. It is hardly surprising that many of the newly freed, subject to the Louverture policies, found their freedom illusory.

To keep the ex-slaves working—to do the same killing labor they had been forced to do before as slaves—took all of Louverture's skill as a leader.[5] In effect, he was carrying out the economic intentions of the French, though with officially recognized freed people. When he learned that the French fleet was bringing General Leclerc and a large army to the island, he surely must have suspected that it was Bonaparte's intention to remove him and reestablish slavery. Yet he fell into the trap. Lured to a meeting, he was taken prisoner, hurried onto a French man-of-war, shipped to France, and confined there at Fort de Joux in the Jura Mountains. It has been said that the French officers who had served under him in Saint Domingue saluted his carriage as it traveled the route along which his captors moved him to prison. He died there, from neglect and pneumonia, within a year.[6]

The Revolution in Haiti, through which Toussaint became so famed that works of art would be created in his memory by Lamartine and by Wordsworth, was won by the revolutionaries after his death. Jean-Jacques Dessalines, another "gilded African" who had served under Louverture but whom the French had failed to capture or kill, declared Haiti's independence on January 1, 1804.[7]

The national struggle of the Republic of Haiti is the only instance in world history in which slaves rose up and successfully wrested the nation itself from those who owned their flesh. The Revolution came to be known in the West as a "nightmare" because the revolutionaries burned plantations and killed people, including many whites. But it also meant the end of slavery there.[8] Afterward, Dessalines said that he had avenged America—with those two words redefining the Revolution. For slaveholding Americans, however, the precise noun for what the Haitians had done was "nightmare." It stood for more than violence. Of course the loudest protests about the Haitian Revolution came from the owners of millions of other humans in the slave societies of the New World tropics, from Tierra del Fuego to the United States. As Dr. Johnson pointed out long ago,[9] slave owners were intensely freedom-loving folk who believed as fiercely in their own freedom as they did in the enslavement of others. The questions for them have always been freedom for whom and freedom from what—questions that have never lost their political relevance.

Reputed to have earned more for France in some years than India had for Britain, a sovereign Haiti sat amid thriving slave-based island plantation enterprises of five major powers—Denmark, the Netherlands, England, France, and Spain—and close to the biggest slave-holding nations of them all: the colony of Brazil (until 1889) at one end and the United States at the other.[10] And Haiti has never escaped either from the images its existence evoked in the West or from the burdens France laid on it after the Revolution. Historians have written about how threatening the newly minted republic of the United States was to Europe's kings. But then something yet more ominous had emerged in America: slaves who had dared to take back their own bodies by force of arms. It was the North Americans' turn—though so recently revolutionary themselves—to be appalled by revolution.

By redeeming their own destinies in the only way they could, the Haitian rebels made a statement about political freedom and about the nature of property. I think of it as an intrinsically modern statement, though the form it took on the ground was anything but a "statement." The National Convention in Paris had abolished slavery in 1794, but it was stamping its approval on what was already happening in the colony. The historian David Geggus calls the decision by the National Convention "surely one of the most radical acts of the entire [French] revolution" (2002:157). Yet it took another nine years for the Haitian people to win what they had been fighting for.

The advance of historical scholarship constantly reassorts what we know; by that reassortment, it can change the meanings of what we know. Yet the fact that the Haitian Revolution was a crucial geopolitical event, one of global importance in "the world" as it was, is still not widely grasped. I think that is not accidental, given how important slavery still was to the West at that time.

Now, two centuries later, it remains difficult to spell out clearly what those desperate hundreds of thousands achieved by their resistance. But for students of that Revolution, surely one thing is clear. Once the fight was fought and won, an enormous collective investment was made by other nations in defining Haiti and its past as falling outside the mainstream of world history (Trouillot 1995). If one sets aside many overtly racist tracts, I think there is not a great deal to suggest a knowing complicity in this concealment. It appears instead to have been the influence of deeply rooted ideas about peoples, civilization, and likeness and difference—indeed, in the way the world was perceived. Still, for nearly two hundred years, many thinkers and writers helped maintain a particular point of view with their silence. Geggus (2002:157–158) points out, for example, how French historians, even in recent years, have continued to ignore the role of "the colonies" in their overview of the French Revolution.

The problem of giving those places and events, now two hundred years passed, their immense and deserved weight is still with us. When it is fully grasped that the three revolutions of the time— American, French, and Haitian—all took place in a relatively brief period and that they were remarkably intermingled, then we see more clearly how endless is the task of trying to sort them out. Needless to add, no such attempt is made here. Yet it may be worth pointing out that whereas the primary sources for the American and French revolutions are vast, those for the Haitian revolution are relatively meager.[11] For quite different reasons, until recently it would have been fair to add that whereas the historical scholarship on the French and American revolutions was similarly vast, that for the Haitian Revolution was correspondingly much more modest.

The purpose of the American Revolution is embodied in this nation's most thrilling and noble document. But the very eloquence of the Declaration of Independence lays bare an enormous gulf between what it says about freedom and to whom it was meant to apply. That unarticulated empty space, that huge question mark, has to do with what was really meant, for those who spoke of them, by "all men" and "inalienable rights." Because of the place of slavery in the fabric of U.S. economic, political, and social life and the aftermath of slavery and Civil War, the United States fell heir to a profound contradiction.

Of the three revolutions, American, French, and Haitian, the Haitian represented the most terrifying reality for its time. To be sure, it was revolutionary in those days to insist on the right to be represented politically if one were taxed; or to deny the absolute rights of monarchy. And many persons gave their lives for their beliefs. But that was not the same as arguing that "human" rights apply to *everyone*—that there was a *universal* definition of who was human—and meaning it. To take that stand would mean, among other things, that the rape, flogging, or sale of someone else's children was a crime, no matter on whom it was inflicted.

Though we cannot be sure they knew it, the Haitian rebels were engaged in an endeavor more radical and more modern even than turning a colony into a sovereign nation. The behavior of the enlightened members of European nobility in regard to the two revolutions, American and Haitian, strikes me as revealing. Those brave men did understand the arguments in favor of independence for the thirteen colonies; many of them staked their lives on the outcome. Lafayette, Pulaski, Rochambeau, and others who flocked to Washington's army risked their lives in a war against European monarchical rule. Yet when the slaves of Saint Domingue were fighting for their freedom under Toussaint, Dessalines, and the other rebels, of course there were no enlightened European noblemen beside them. It was not that the primary aim of the Haitian revolutionaries was difficult to grasp. It was that even among Europe's democratically minded nobility, universal human equality was still an abstract idea the ramifications of which were not understood. No Rochambeau or Lafayette could imagine joining the masses of African born rebels to fight for it.[12]

Of the three revolutions, French, American, and Haitian—and not forgetting that the French Revolution had abolished slavery, at least for a time—only the Haitian Revolution ended slavery. Haiti's people paid indemnities to France to win diplomatic recognition and to forestall reinvasion; haggling over the price of freedom went on for years. In 1825 France agreed at last to recognize Haiti's sovereignty, since Haiti's president, Jean Pierre Boyer, had agreed to the indemnity payments. They were at first ƒ150,000,000 (later reduced to ƒ60,000,000), to be paid over a five-year period. In effect, the Haitian people were obliged to pay for the past and future value of their labor and, indeed, to buy themselves and their children. (When Boyer signed the agreement, there were fourteen French warships in the Port-au-Prince harbor.) The Vatican, cautious about the international implications of its actions, refused to sign a concordat with Haiti until 1860, though the nation was (or had been) mostly Catholic. The United States did not (indeed, given its reliance on slavery, could not) recognize Haiti until 1862, nearly sixty years after Haiti won its independence. The very idea of a black political diplomat from a sovereign state (especially one that had ended slavery by the sword) being officially received in our national capital enraged the slaveholding constituents of southern congressmen. Political ostracism is both a form of punishment and a very old solution for political embarrassment.

The very idea of an independent country full of people whose lives and bodies had belonged to others and who had regained their freedom by acts of violence was an international reproach to every owner of slaves, but that was not the way it was perceived. Slave owners must surely have prayed for Haiti's destruction. Yet for the slaves, the Revolution did not come a moment too soon; and there remains little doubt that its reality advanced the cause of freedom elsewhere in the hemisphere (Genovese 1992; Scott 1986). It made clear to slaves in other places and even to some slaveholders that freedom could be won by violent resistance. Though it was still remote, the prescient could even imagine the eventual end of all New World plantation slavery. It was almost exactly eight decades before that happened.

The Haitian Revolution played some part in Napoleon's decision, after Leclerc's defeat and death, to negotiate the Louisiana Purchase (Dubois 2004:304). Events in Europe and in the United States might have one day brought it about in any case. But with the loss of Saint Domingue, France's readiness to defend a mainland colony next to the United States declined. The Purchase facilitated the consolidation of a continental United States, a process helped along by the revolutionaries of Haiti—a favor for which no one has ever thanked them.[13]

This is certainly not to say that the people of Haiti, having won their freedom, would prosper under enlightened and democratic rule—far from it. That so valiant a people in war should be so persistently frustrated in peace is seen as mysterious or ironical. The establishment of Haitian sovereignty at the end of the Revolution was in its own way as astonishing as victory itself. Most of the people who had led the Revolution were illiterate; many of the soldiers and more than half of the Haitian people at the time had been born in Africa. Louverture himself was born in the colony and exemplifies the talent and energy of the revolutionary leaders. Most of his fellow generals were less educated than he.

The leaders who survived him faced terrible difficulties. Much of the basic infrastructure of the colony on which the new nation would have to be established had been ruined during fourteen years of war, and few ground-level organizations such as schools had ever been established there for "ordinary" people. Plantation societies like Saint Domingue, built on massed slave labor, lacked many of the institutions that grow up around the activities of free people. Though Cap Français, Saint Domingue's principal city, was as large as Boston and boasted theaters, glittering entertainments, a lively press, political and social clubs, and schools (Dubois 2004:21–24), these were for the free and, to a lesser extent, the freed.[14] For the slaves no newspapers, schools, hospitals—and of course no political institutions. No money was spent on the elevation of the slaves.

In contrast to Haiti, the United States—in revolt after 1776, with only parts of its economy plantation based—began life with no doubt the largest percentage of college graduates of any country in history. It benefited from the gradual restoration of links of all sorts with Britain once the Revolution ended. Speaking the same language, almost entirely Christian, bound by much the same culture and myriad familial relationships, the enormous political differences between the peoples of the United Kingdom and the United States did not negate shared traditions or divorce the two nations from each other. The United States was able to maintain its warm ties with France as well, ties that had grown stronger during the American Revolution.

Not so Haiti. Europe, much like the Americans, obdurately refused to see Haiti as an authentic nation, let alone a new or equal one. Isolated precisely because they had won their freedom, Haitians now saw some aspects of the prerevolutionary social order reappear in their country, though now there were few Europeans or whites left. Power lay primarily with the army's leaders, some of them drawn from the *gens de couleur,* the free colored. Many or most of these people were better educated than the newly freed masses, among whom a large majority were African born. Some of the *gens de couleur* had been educated in France. Many were lighter in color than most of the newly freed. Importantly, by the 1790s, some of the *gens de couleur* were a second, third, or even fourth generation removed from their slave ancestors (Leyburn 1966:17).[15]

Observers have stressed the color differences between these people and the ex-slaves in the evolving form of postrevolutionary Haitian society. I do not discount the potentially powerful significance of those differences. Yet I think the social, cultural, and educational differences between freed persons and their descendants and the newly freed ex-slaves were (or would one day become) at least equally important. In the nineteenth century, those differences would be perpetuated in some regards, such as rural-urban distinctions, and even deepened.

Many historians now see that the French and Haitian revolutions were intricately connected, just as had been the histories of the countries within which they evolved, one the colonial master, the other the colony itself. In the case of French Saint Domingue, a central feature of its society—as in some other Caribbean colonies—had been the emergence and inflection of social categories between the slaves on the one hand and the white French planters on the other. The white planters, or *grand blancs,* represented an extension of French power. The slaves, of course, were in a category fixed by law. But French law, embodied in the Code Noir of 1685, had instituted opportunities for slaves to become free and for freed persons to enjoy rights not matched in other Caribbean slave-based colonies.[16] The most important source of freedom there, as elsewhere, arose originally through the cohabitation of white and nonwhite.

I am unable to describe fully here the complex social differentiation that unfolded in French Saint Domingue between 1697, when it became French by treaty, and the outbreak of revolution in France in 1789.[17] A number of excellent historical studies of Saint Dominique and emergent Haiti (among others, Dubois 2004; Fick 1990; Garrigus 2006; Gaspar and Garrigus 1997; Geggus 2002) have done so. That social differentiation turned on the increasing numbers of persons who were neither black nor slaves and the increasing wealth (but without commensurate political power) of those persons. Terms such as *gens de couleur, affranchis, libres,* and others have been used to describe these people. They did not form a single group or class, economically, socially, or politically—nor were the most dis-

tinguished among them simply French citizens who happened not
to be perceived as white. Some, three or four generations removed
from slavery, had great wealth and some influence, owned slaves
and plantations, saw themselves as French, and were proslavery in
outlook. A great many others were the children of two free persons
at least one of whom was "not white." Hence it would be misleading to treat all of Saint Domingue's people who were neither white
nor slave as one politically or economically homogeneous category.
Yet it is difficult, if not impossible, to give an accurate account of
the entangled histories of France and Saint Domingue and the place
of these "people of color" in that history without saying more
about them. Geggus states the case clearly:

> Saint Domingue's free nonwhite population was unusual for
> its size and, more particularly, its wealth. Except in the Iberian
> colonies, free people of color were generally a very small minor-
> ity. Very rarely did they rise above the position of prosperous
> artisan. In Saint Domingue, however, the *gens de couleur libres*
> outnumbered the whites in two of the colony's three provinces,
> and they included in their number rich and cultivated planters
> who had been educated in France. In Saint Domingue, anyone
> with a black ancestor, no matter how remote, was subject to the
> humiliating legal discrimination typical of all slave colonies in
> the eighteenth century. Nonwhites were banned from public of-
> fice and the professions and were forbidden to wear fine cloth-
> ing, to carry weapons in town, to sit with whites in church,
> at the theatre, or when eating. They were not only unequal be-
> fore the law but also suffered extralegal harassment, especially

from poor whites with whom they competed for jobs. (Geggus
2002:6)

The *gens de couleur* thus covered an extremely broad social range,
from recently freed African slaves to rich landowners and tradesper-
sons who were almost indistinguishable in appearance or culture
from their white counterparts. They constituted merely a legal category (those who were neither slave nor white) rather than a class.
Probably a majority of the men were artisans or smallholders. The
women were usually petty traders or white men's mistresses. As
most were of mixed racial descent, the term "mulatto" was sometimes applied to the entire nonwhite free community. Some had
both whites and slaves for relatives. The position of free people of
color in Saint Domingue society was therefore highly ambiguous.
Many were slave owners or hunted down fugitive slaves in the militia and rural police force. All were held in subjection by the whites.

Despite the spread of liberal ideas in Europe, the laws governing
free nonwhites in France as well as Saint Domingue grew increasingly severe in the late eighteenth century—a paradox of the French
Enlightenment. At the same time, the free coloreds grew rapidly in
number and in wealth as they profited from the coffee boom. From
the 1780s, they not only dominated the rural police force but in addition formed the backbone of the colonial militia (Geggus 2002:6–7).

We know that the status of these free *gens de couleur* differed sig-
nificantly over time, and varied regionally, owing largely to differences in landowning, crops grown, numbers, and other factors
(Garrigus 2006; Geggus 2002; Trouillot 1982). But while regional
variation mattered greatly, it should not obscure two solid facts

about the social status of people who were neither slaves nor white in Saint Dominique in the eighteenth century. First, among them were many who were prosperous, and some very wealthy, by any standard. Second, though they certainly had not coalesced into a political bloc in regard to their own rights on the basis of color, the most successful among them had become vigorous defenders of those rights.

In less than a century—between 1697, when Saint Domingue was officially ceded to France by Spain, and the beginnings of revolt in 1789–91—the nonwhite and free became an economic and social force to be reckoned with. By 1789 they were almost as numerous as the whites, and ample evidence—especially as reflected in the legal and social pressures to which they were eventually subjected—demonstrates that their influence on local life was substantial.[18] All this, despite Geggus's fair conclusion that "all were held in subjection by whites."

One need not look far to find a persuasive—yet I would insist only partial—explanation for this situation. As Leyburn (1966:16–20) noted long ago, Louis XIV's Code Noir of 1685 had set forth the laws intended to govern race and class relations in Saint Domingue and other colonies. The Code declared that slaves, once freed, had rights nearly the same as those of French citizens. They could own land, travel freely, testify in a court of law (and against whites), marry freely, and own slaves. Importantly, the Code also stipulated that freed persons had the right to endow their children with property and wealth. Under these laws, many free colored inherited, were given, bought, or married into wealth in land and slaves; many spent time in France, and some lived there. Tellingly, they served, often as officers, in the militias of Saint Domingue. Yet their rights were not exactly the same as French citizens'; and over time they faced increasing impediments.

Although before the 1760s the Code was imperfectly observed and there were pressures against it on the part of some of the whites, it made possible the rise of the *gens de couleur*. Garrigus (2006) and Dubois (2004) provide detailed evidence that the way the free colored first rose in the social system of Saint Domingue was as the children of "mixed" unions whose paternity was recognized through marriage and who then often became inheritors of land and other wealth. Dubois notes: "Some [whites] freed the women [by whom they fathered children] and married them, as the Code Noir stipulated whites who had children with slaves should do. Many whites left land and slaves to their partners and children. Indeed it was generally expected that they would do so, and Saint-Domingue whites resisted royal attempts to institute laws outlawing such bequests. As a result, a class of property-owning free people of color emerged in the colony" (62).

But as the political situation in France worsened after the Seven Years' War, the civil rights of the *gens de couleur* were subjected to enormous pressure and declined in the colony (and in France itself). Whites both rich and poor increasingly strove to assert their superiority to the free colored, on grounds of physical difference and origin, successfully passing legislation that restricted the rights of the free colored to own land and slaves. Their efforts met with heated resistance. The free colored were zealous in defending their rights as Frenchmen, including of course their property rights in land and slaves, as had their ancestors before them.[19] More and more, the laws took aim at those rights: laws against taking the name of one's former master (or white relatives), laws against the practice of law or medicine, and so on. As the restrictions increased, so did the contradictoriness of the social situation, as Dubois points out:

> Even as laws meant to limit the power and numbers of free people of color proliferated, whites continued to have sexual relationships with women of African descent, both slave and free, *and to give their partners and children property and slaves.* . . . Whites were connected to free people of color by a complex web of familial and social ties; men of European and African descent were, often literally, "sons of the same father." And yet the law created a difference between them. . . . Saint-Domingue was a schizophrenic society in which the law attacked relationships between those of European and African descent *even as whites who supported such laws continuously flouted them.* (2004:68; italics added)

Though the *gens de couleur* were not the ideological opponents of the white masters on the rightness of slavery itself, in that they wanted most of all to be treated as Frenchmen and as the equals of slaveholding white Frenchmen, they were now increasingly viewed as threatening and dangerous by the whites. In view of the power the free colored did wield and what they were doing to defend themselves, it is probably not surprising that many of the French-born and white turned on their neighbors (at times upon their relatives). Garrigus (2006) thinks the white planters in Saint Domingue were deeply insecure about the opinions that their fellow citizens in France had of them. If their animus toward the *gens de couleur* arose from this, he reasons, they would feel strongly the need to make clear to those at home that they were as French, and as white, as

Parisians. If the white planters in Saint Domingue feared Parisians might mistake one of them for one of the free colored, a new 1779 law (Dubois 2004:62) making it illegal for the people of color even to copy the clothing styles or the coiffures of the whites of Saint Domingue seems slightly less bizarre.[20]

But despite the assault on in their rights and privileges, on the eve of the Revolution the free colored were continuing to increase or at least to maintain their wealth and status (Garrigus 2006:172). At that time, Fick writes (in Gaspar and Geggus 1997:56), the *gens de couleur* "owned one-third of the colony's plantations, one-quarter of the slaves, and one-quarter of the real estate property."[21] Leyburn's figures differ slightly: "Some say that in 1791 they owned a third of all the land and a fourth of all the slaves; others more conservative put the figure at one fifth each" (1966:18). Garrigus (37) notes that "Julien Raimond, a free colored planter, thought the *gens de couleur* controlled one fourth of the profits of the Saint Domingue colony." Though these are only estimates, they suggest that 20–25 percent of all of the slaves may have been owned by *gens de couleur*. That is, of the slightly more than 450,000 slaves in the colony, between 90,000 and 110,000 were owned by nonwhite slaveholders.

The implications of the waxing alienation between whites and *gens de couleur* in the colony are many, among them one that relates to the Revolution itself. I think that without the bitter and divisive struggle between the whites and the free colored, the Revolution would probably not have succeeded.[22] The consequences of leaving wealth to "mixed" children, made possible at the outset by the Code Noir, and undertaken by the first generation of French planters, had now arisen to divide them. The white planters were busy with the political implications of the French Revolution for their future and their property. But they found time to quarrel over what any of their nonwhite neighbors wore and how they styled their coiffures as well. In 1791, in the middle of the tantrums of the *grands blancs,* the slaves—the half-forgotten, ever-present half million whose daily suffering had created the wealth of Saint Domingue—revolted. What was put in motion then could not be halted.

But looking back at the emergence of the free colored in the colony, it is impossible not to wonder at the singularity and importance of their history there. In no other slave society of the Caribbean did so visible and assertive an emancipatory process take shape—all the more remarkable because it happened year by year as plantation slavery itself grew into the colony's regnant social fact. As vital as the Code Noir was in making possible some of the major potential features of the colonial social system a century later, I do not think it wholly explains the remarkable upward mobility of the *gens de couleur.* The Code Noir specified individual obligations and rights. The white colonists complied with (and in the face of enormous pressure, apparently *continued* to comply with) its stipulations.

My having tried in earlier work to understand Jamaica's past led me to look at work by historians on the ways the power and status of the *gens de couleur* had gradually taken shape in Saint Domingue. There is a solid historical likeness between the colonies of Jamaica and Saint Domingue. These two premier slave-based sugar islands of the seventeenth century were the largest and the most profitable Caribbean dependencies in the history of their respective metropolises. They both grew swiftly in population—especially slave population—economic activity, and lucrativeness from the latter decades of the seventeenth century to those of the eighteenth. Yet they differed sharply in their evolving social composition and, I think, may have differed as well in the attached values of their planter classes.

In Jamaica, from the first—that is, in the decades following the British seizure of the island—no significant propertied or politically influential class of mixed-race persons ever emerged.[23] No legal concessions were made to those born of "mixed-race"; none was ever made to nonwhite freed persons as a group or class. According to the Jamaican courts, manumission was "nothing more than the abandonment or release of property authority"; it gave no rights beyond freedom (Edwards 1793, 2:133). That is not to say that "evolving" from being the son of a slave mother to being a free white male slave owner was impossible. But there it took at least four generations, a series of fortunate marriages involving whites, and immense good fortune. In his classic study *Creole Society in Jamaica, 1770-1820* (2005:188), Brathwaite refers to a legal marriage of a free white Jamaican quadroon male *"to a white woman"*; his use of italics for the phrase suggests, as he makes clear, that the event was only barely imaginable.[24] Heuman (1981:13) writes of Jamaicans James Swaby and Thomas Drummond, who were free colored wealthy estate and slave owners. But at best they remain astonishing exceptions. The genealogical obsession with who was white, who wasn't, and how much, resonates with what has happened in all of the other places in the world where people have been driven close to madness by the difference between categories on paper and the living social biology of our perennially fertile species.[25]

Yet, while much of the same cruel nonsense was to be found in Saint Domingue, the free colored there early obtained for themselves a solid stake in the society, deformed as it was, and set out to defend it. How else are we able to explain the estimated one-quarter of the slaves and one-quarter of the real estate they are thought to have owned?

Such an outcome was unthinkable in Jamaica. There, from the start of the British colony, free colored persons had to petition the Jamaica Assembly individually for specific privileges, such as the right to testify in court. Hurwitz and Hurwitz (1967:425, 429) recorded 128 of those petitions in Jamaica, the total submitted over the course of one hundred years (1700–1800). The Assembly granted all of the rights of whites, such as officeholding, to only four petitioners out of those 128. The other petitions were either denied or the petitioners were admitted only to specific limited rights. But right up to emancipation, and one could argue well beyond, the Jamaica Assembly was zealously on guard against anything that might empower colored free people. There were special efforts, in meeting any appeal, to divide the wealthier colored from those who were free and had less and to impugn the motives of all of the free colored.

Contemporary with the mounting pressure for new legal constraints on the free colored in Saint Domingue, the mid-eighteenth century also saw more laws enacted to control the free colored in Jamaica. The "legacy limitation act" of 1761, for example, specified that "no land, cattle, slaves, money or real estate in excess of £200 be granted to any Negro whatsoever, or to any mulatto or other persons, even if born in lawful wedlock" (Hurwitz and Hurwitz 1967:425, 429). Hall (1972:206) gives evidence of systematic, legally sustained discrimination against any access to property or power by the nonwhite free.

I have noted that a powerful movement to restrict the rights of the free colored arose in French Saint Domingue as well. But it arose in the context of an already existing group many of whom had both wealth and some of whom had—though quite circumscribed—political clout. Why were the cases so different? Fundamentally, I think it was because—as noted—the Saint Domingue sugar planters, during the expanding decades of the sugar boom there, seemed much readier to recognize and protect, and often to legitimize by marriage, their mixed-race children. Without the readiness of white French males to free and marry the slave mothers who bore their children, to protect and educate those children, and to make them their rightful heirs, the *gens de couleur* would have more closely resembled the people like them in Jamaica.

In Jamaica, the male offspring of white planters and female slaves were sometimes protected by their fathers, even if they could not be legally protected. Some were also educated by their fathers. But though the size of the free colored group in Jamaica was similar to that of Saint Domingue and though, as we have seen, it did include at least a few colored slave owners, only in rare exceptions did they become persons of propertied wealth.

If there was any difference between these two master classes, it was surely not in their sexuality. It was, rather, in their conceptions of family: their affective perceptions of the reality of their own flesh and blood. The feelings they had about their own bloodline must have deeply influenced how they behaved toward their own children. To put it in admittedly too simple a way, I think in eighteenth-century Jamaica, race usually trumped blood; in eighteenth-century Saint Domingue, blood sometimes won out over race.

What set apart the behavior of the white planters of Saint Domingue who empowered their colored children and their slave mothers had to do with kinship, I think. To be sure, it would not have taken on its social dimensions without the Code Noir; and by the middle of the eighteenth century, the struggle of the *gens de couleur* for civil equality with the whites threatened to shake the whole system of power. But there is nothing in human affairs more intimate than how people classify and acknowledge those to whom they recognize that they are related, namely kinship, and it was the form of kinship ties that distinguished the Haitian case from the Jamaican.

Political and economic forces came into deadly play in this story. By 1789, whatever the Code Noir had originally prescribed had been rewritten into behavior and into the population. Some of its stipulations were forgotten, others bitterly regretted—at least by many whites in Saint Domingue. But in the meantime the free colored had come to be perceived as a threat to the existing order. If we recall Geggus's (2002:6) matter-of-fact observation: "Some had both whites and slaves for relatives"—the poignancy and potential horror of the situation is borne in on us.

Over time, some of the values expressed in the Code Noir, including those shaping kinship ties, grew weaker. But it seems to me that the earlier rise of the *gens de couleur* had turned importantly on the qualities expressed in one of humankind's oldest devices for ordering social relations: the concepts of marriage and parenthood and their legitimation.

It was amid the fierce politicking and struggles of white planters and *gens de couleur* that the slaves took matters into their own hands. And if there be irony in this interpretation, it is that the Revolution had become a reality at least in part because some of the French slave owners had tried from the beginnings of the colony to raise their children, including those by slave mothers, to think just like themselves.

The most important economic change in Haiti after the Revolution was the eventual destruction of the plantations and the end of sugar as an export commodity. The survivors of those half-million slaves whose labor had powered sugar plantations and coffee estates, making Saint Domingue one of the most lucrative European colonies in history, were now free. And like the Jamaican people, what they wanted above all was land. Fick says it well: "a personal claim to the land upon which one labored and from which to derive and express one's individuality was, for the black laborers, a necessary and an essential element in their vision of freedom. For without this concrete economic and social reality, freedom for the ex-slaves was little more than a legal abstraction" (1990:249). But those desires were at first frustrated, despite their free status. It may seem incongruous that the generals who had led the slaves to freedom should have attempted to keep the plantations going. But in the tradition of Louverture, they did. Henry Christophe vainly used coercion to this end in the north until his death. In the south, Governor Dessalines— later Emperor Jacques I—did the same (Fick 2000:29–33) but to no avail.

In the south, in the regime of free colored ex-general Alexandre Pétion, one of the greatest plantation colonies in history began its transformation into the New World's most solidly peasant country. Nearly every particle of Haitian sugar thereafter would be eaten by the Haitians themselves—in the form of the molasses-colored "logs" called *rapadou* (Sp. *raspadura*)—wrapped picturesquely in banana leaves. Only a few animal-driven mills were still operating by the 1830s.[26] Not until the U.S. Occupation did factory-ground sugar reappear in Haiti—in 1922, on one small plantation in the north.

Pétion's quite unintended "land reform" began around 1809, with modest grants of as few as fifteen acres to veterans in lieu of wages owed, more to men of higher ranks. Fick (2000) indicates that the choicest land went to those intending to produce export commodities. But some 400,000 acres went to officers, civil servants and even "influential politicians"—a total of 10,000 such grants between 1810 and 1817. Both rental and sharecropping became common. After the suicide of Henri Christophe in 1820, this policy was extended to the north by his successor, Jean-Pierre Boyer. The rise of the peasantry coincided with the end of the plantation. It emphatically did not mean peasant equality; there always were rich and poor and landless peasants. But it did mean a gradual postrevolutionary transformation of Haitian economy and society, which turned in large measure on the state's inability any longer to tie down a free people and siphon off enough of their labor power to make the exaction worthwhile in that form. In Jamaica, the decline of planter power after abolition was grudging and less thoroughgoing. In Puerto Rico the plantation system itself had already been in some decline by the time slavery ended in 1876. But in Haiti, the world's biggest sugar-producing economy had been reduced to ashes in a few years. Haiti retained its agricultural self-sufficiency but not its place in the world economy. This self-sufficiency rested ultimately on the proto-peasant production that had flourished earlier.

Fick writes:

> The plantation system that had been the cornerstone of the former colony and the source of its tremendous wealth was now in

irreversible ruin. Even Christophe, by the end of his reign, could not have kept it going much longer in the face of mounting resistance. But what this also meant was that Haiti was no longer a player of any significance in the Atlantic economy. And, although the parcelling of land that Pétion initiated in the early years of his presidency and that ended by defining the rural land structure of nineteenth-century Haiti may have helped to hasten the collapse of the plantation system and accelerate the economic decline of the country, it enabled the post-independence Haitian masses to define their freedom. For the rural peasantry of Haiti it was the internal logic of the revolution from below that triumphed, even if it meant individual freedom in poverty. (2000:35)

Numerous prerevolutionary market places, supplied and patronized by thousands of slave cultivators who produced both their subsistence and the surpluses they sold in market on their own time, had been one of the few institutions built around slave initiative and talent in Saint Domingue. After victory they continued to function in spite of the destruction and disorder of the Revolution. In his famous book on the colony, written after he had fled, Moreau de St. Méry (1797) described glowingly the Clugny marketplace in Cap Français where 15,000 slaves marketed each Sunday (Dayan 1995). Dayan points out that this participation by the slaves was actually prohibited by the Code Noir. In Saint Domingue as in Jamaica, "custom" had prevailed over unenforced law. The proto-peasants had patiently negotiated their opportunities, no matter how barbaric and oppressive the system, until freedom was finally won.

By the 1820s, peasant cultivators had established their farms *(lakou),* which were organized around the labor of their wives and sons, and lived in patrilineal, patrilocal extended family groups, producing a major part of their daily needs. They sold their surpluses through the market system and could reach the world market with their coffee. The similarities to and differences from Jamaica are striking. While the family land tradition in Jamaica has some resemblance to the Haitian one, Jamaica seems never to have had extended families in large homesteads. The history of land there was of course quite different. Still, the Jamaican institution of family land provides a quite striking parallel to the *lakou* (Besson 2002); and Jamaica did develop a large (though predominantly smallholding) peasantry.

Holt (1992:347–365) shows how, long after Morant Bay, in the early days when bananas were becoming one of the pioneer perishable imports to the United States, 80 percent of those bananas were coming from Jamaican smallholders. That new, foreign opportunity for peasants with only smallholdings but lots of energy and zeal provided wealth and stability, at least for a couple of decades. The period after Morant Bay had seen a large increase in small farms; and from the 1870s through the 1890s, the Jamaican peasant cultivator—albeit always on a small scale—did well. A former Jamaica governor, Sir Anthony Musgrave, insisted that contrary to the opinion in Britain, Jamaica's government revenues came more from smallholders than from any other sector, including sugar (338). The banana export trade was giving peasants the chance to show what they were capable of. But the Colonial Office did nothing to help the peasantry beyond taxing them. Soon enough, the bananas and other fruits becoming popular in the temperate world would be brought within the domain of corporate shippers in Europe and the United States. Their capital and influence would help to turn many Jamaican peasants—as well as those on the mainland of Central America—into wage workers. The era of the "banana republic" had arrived.

In the Haitian case, before population growth, land erosion, and the effects of equal inheritance slowed down the economy, the ancestral homes of the Haitian peasantry not only were economic units but also became centers of extended family religious worship and ancestral burying grounds. The state's original grants were as large as thirty-six acres in some cases. Toward the end of the nineteenth century, though, such joint-family holdings had already begun to degenerate, mostly because of equal inheritance and land subdivision, as population grew. Yet for at least a century, Haiti was where a genuine reconstituted peasant existence probably came closest to fulfillment in this hemisphere.

Coffee cultivation there had been next after sugar in importance before the Revolution. It became the chief export afterward, now produced by a free peasantry. In many places, the nature of sugar-cane and the demands its processing impose on the producer have usually led toward large-scale enterprise and the unity of cultivation and processing. But if the time constraints in the growing and cutting of cane can be successfully separated from the processing, then smallholders are able to produce the raw material to be processed by central mills. Scott (1985, 2005) has shown how this happened in Cuba, and it would also become practice in Jamaica. In Haiti, as in these other islands, the history of coffee has always been connected to small producers. After the Revolution, that association became even more pronounced.

Other exports, including oil-yielding plants, goatskins and goat horns, bone for buttons, honey, and essential oils such as vetiver and beeswax, have long been produced for sale there. When I was doing fieldwork there in the 1950s, coffee buyers from the city regularly set up their stands near the marketplaces and trucked their bulk purchases from the countryside to ports of embarkation.[27]

These were the products of a people who had little opportunity earlier to learn manufacturing skills or advanced crafts. They made baskets, trays, and wooden stools for themselves and for local markets, and at a later time the countryside boasted smiths, tanners, cobblers, and furniture makers, eventually even tinsmiths and tailors.[28] By 1830 Haiti was no longer a plantation colony making sugar, rum, and molasses for French consumers. It had become a poor but relatively peaceful farming economy.[29] That economy sustained a large, socially differentiated peasant population—rich peasants, poor peasants, and landless people working for the landed. Uneducated, rural, and—to use words not often applied to them— quite individualistic, Haiti's nineteenth-century peasantry was to become, more and more, the fair game of its own elite.

As the Revolution ended and civil order was restored, free Haiti's ruling class began looking for ways to exact from the people the fruits of their labor. In Haiti that was not so easy to do as it might sound. Like peasantries everywhere, the Haitian country folk produced most of what they consumed and wasted little. But there are things a peasantry feels it must have and can not produce—school notebooks, iron tools, kerosene lamps, china—as well as their "ceremonial" needs, as Wolf (1966) labeled them, for some of which there are no substitutes. We need to be reminded that even poor people have important standards to be kept of how to live a proper life. For those things, peasants must turn to the wider world. Every link to the market that a peasant needs in order to live the way that he wants, or the way state power makes him live, can be made into an instrument with which to exact a portion of his productivity. In the case of peasants' products for sale, the terms of trade can be turned against them by fiat. Persons in the Haitian ruling group became experts in exaction.

Petty bureaucrats, coffee exporters, lawyers, military officers and merchants—intermediaries of all sorts—soon contrived to rest their collective weight on the backs of the peasantry. Most of the merchants retreated to the towns. Poor and landless peasants were bullied by other peasants richer or better connected than they. Yet I think that probably for a century, the Haitian people lived far better than they could have imagined when they had been slaves— indeed, far better than peasants in most of the Andes or Mexico and Central America, where big landowners had kept their power. But they were ill served by regimes that aimed at siphoning off their productivity and routinizing the exaction of their effort. That aspect of the picture has never changed, and I think that it never will in Haiti, unless its ruling class is reined in by external power (Mintz 1995). The peasantry, meanwhile, is now greatly weakened and diminished.

My Jamaican and Puerto Rican experiences had made me interested in how market systems function in peasant societies. I had done some work on peasant marketplaces in Jamaica (1955, 1957, 1978) and knew that such marketplaces were even more important in Haiti, where there were hardly any stores outside the large towns. The colonial connection to France ended in 1804. The diplomatic intimidation afterward made reconstruction of civil society more difficult and any commercial growth far weaker. Trade by sea continued, both along Haiti's coasts and with Santo Domingo, as well as with neighboring islands. The internal economy continued to develop.

I made my first visit to Haiti in 1957 and began my fieldwork there in the summer of the following year. I hoped to find out how the internal market system functioned and what purposes it served in the national economy. I recalled how Julian Steward, who had sent a group of us student anthropologists to Puerto Rico to apply our methods to the analysis of a national society had encouraged us to think seriously about how national institutions work.

I am using the word "institution" pretty loosely here. I mean it to refer primarily to a practice that is usually regulated socially—a visible and normative practice, not a familial or private one; a practice connected to some basic social need such as, say, economic cooperation or political organization or collective religious belief. The family is an institution; but cooperative work groups, churches, and even courtship practices can also be institutions (see also Chapter 5).

In the case of Haiti, it was my impression that after the Revolution, and except for the military, there were hardly any functioning institutions that were linked to the national government. This thin institutional structure may be an index of governmental weakness, perhaps also of poverty. I have referred to this deficiency already. There had been many institutions for the free before the Revolution (McClellan 1992). But once the plantations were gone, the countryside had little else. Schools, hospitals, fire departments, local governing bodies—even roads—were in large measure absent. But if this is true, it means that after freedom, the things that tied the Haitian people to the national center of power were few and weak. The happy absence of colonial power was matched by the not-so-happy absence of roads, schools, and hospitals in the countryside. As I prepared to do fieldwork there, I kept in mind the many new American nations, as in Latin America, all of which had had to construct new systems of governance. Haiti was similar, but there the colonial government had been ousted early. I clearly remember, once I'd become accustomed to the countryside, thinking about how Haiti was bereft of an institutional structure because it had thrown out the French and had had little opportunity to learn how to create one of its own. Because of its special and violent history, only a small minority of its population had been affected by the culture of the now-vanished French colonial masters.

For a different but equally important reason, an institutional structure adequate to deal with the needs of a newly sovereign and independent people failed to develop. The colonial society had been organized around, and by means of, the sugar plantations, even though coffee farms, usually enterprises run by families (and often interracial) with a few slaves, had become more and more important. Plantation societies require a centralized government to provide adequate ports, military protection, slave-catching bodies, and jails, but not so many schools, hospitals, agricultural extension agencies and banks. The slow and very imperfect development of institutions after 1804 owed partly to the plantation past, soon to be blotted out by a burgeoning free peasant society.

In Haiti, the peasants everywhere practice a religion called vodoun or "voodoo." It was not a research subject that had won my interest; but the social functions of vodoun intrigued me. Vodoun is a national religion in Haiti, as is Catholicism. The nature of and relationship between these two belief systems has been of interest to many scholars. But unlike Catholicism, vodoun has no national institutional structure or hierarchy. Nor is it eager to proselytize, except for a few opportunistic, cult-like freelancers. Nationally important because so many Haitians share belief in at least some of its ideas even if of different class backgrounds, vodoun lacks organizational attributes associated with religions in, say, the United States or Europe. There is no ancestral text, no hierarchy, no seminary, no missionaries, no uniforms—no bingo, no summer camps, no heavy engagement with depicting God or his son as a goodfella or an Anglo-Saxon pitchman. More like a collection of cults all of whose members believe in much the same things without much regard to any local leader except their very own, it exists and is important nationally, and I consider it an institution. But even if it is, I do not think of it as a *national* institution, because there exist no working structural connections among its parts.

One of vodoun's strongest rallying points in the twentieth century, long after Rome finally decided to forgive the Haitian people for their success in driving out their rulers in 1804, was the "anti-superstition" campaigns the Church promoted against it in the 1930s. A staggering treasure of drums and other ceremonial objects was burned and destroyed.[30] Yet Haiti has remained a nation with a national religion called Catholicism and a Haitian religion called vodoun.

Though many tyrants have ruled Haiti, except for the *chefs de section*, local political and quasijudicial bosses linked to the state (Comhaire 1955; Lahav 1975; Moral 1978; Sheller 2000), the villages of Haiti can hardly be said to be tied by anything to national leadership, beyond the military itself. The military is immensely important. But there is little else of a national sort to be found in the countryside. To this day, outside a few towns and the capital, national institutions in Haiti are poorly represented by any local-level links. Such familiar places as banks, post offices, hospitals—not to mention schools, power plants, garbage dumps, government vehicles—are both scarce and meagerly sustained.

When I began to work in Haiti, I wondered whether the market system might really be the only truly *national* institution, beyond the army. Let me describe the market system briefly. At the time that I did my fieldwork in Haiti in 1958-59, eight out of ten Haitians were peasants. Most of them produced their own subsistence—without gas generators, running water, kerosene stoves, or electricity. They were doing it in a country that had—outside the towns—no paved roads, transport or postal service, schools, hospitals, active agricultural extension, or information media (except gossip—what they themselves refer to humorously as *télédyòl*, loosely translatable as "tele-mouth").[31] In spite of being heavily taxed in every way that an idle, cruel, and cunning state apparatus could think up, the peasantry—illiterate, submissive, unschooled, lacking medical care—fed itself fairly well, reproduced itself, maintained stable family life, and supported on its back the entire state apparatus, including the army.

There must be few countries in the world—Haiti unfortunately has competitors—where such a mass of bureaucrats is supported by so poor a peasantry while supplying in return neither help nor security, advice or protection, and not even—as far as I saw—much friendliness and respect. I consider this to be part of the very high price the Haitian people were required to pay when they became an independent country. Even colonialism in Africa—surely no bargain for any local people—provided some institutional continuity. But fourteen years of invasion, revolution, and war waged on the terrain of a huge slave-based economy meant that Haiti's institutional slate would be wiped nearly entirely clean by 1804.

Against that depressing past, the internal market system, by which all of the agricultural produce of the countryside and much else destined for local use would reach its consumers, touches every city, town, and rural district in Haiti. The marketplaces numbered in the hundreds. When I was working there, over 54,000 licensed intermediaries plied their skills across the land. All produce for export reached the ports through bulk buyers whose activities grew up alongside the market system and were closely allied to it. The commission buyers who lined the road near a market I studied in 1958–1959 purchased raw produce for export—vetiver, beeswax, goatskins, coffee—from peasants who came to town to sell their products and to shop at the marketplace before returning home. Especially important was coffee—a high-quality, mild variety that went mostly to Germany, France, and Switzerland and was used in mixed blends.[32] Nearly every one of the intermediaries, known in Haiti by various terms—*révâdèz, kòmèsâ, machâ, Madâm Sara* (this last after an extremely noisy bird that clusters in the trees to chatter)—according to their varying roles, is female. It was common to see three or four daughters, all dressed identically (at that time, blue denim dress and orange head tie), walking single file behind their mother to market, each with a load of appropriate size on her head. Marketing is to Haitian females as farming is to Jamaican males. Though there are women who cultivate and men who market, the division of labor is real; it is a key to understanding how Haitian peasants deal with the economics of everyday life. Women hardly cultivate for the same reason that men hardly market, and each task carries particular social messages.

Which brings me to my friend Nana, a market woman from Duverger, in the fifth rural section of Anse-à-Veau, near the border with Acquin in the southern peninsula, near the marketplace of

Fonds-des-Nègres. Planning my fieldwork, I had decided to pick a large regional marketplace in the north of Haiti to study, and another in the south, since the cultural differences between the regions are substantial. In the south, I visited several markets before settling on Fonds-des-Nègres, which had Tuesday as its major market day. Fonds-des-Nègres is not located in a town; town markets are controlled to some extent by local businesses, because marketers do not go elsewhere to buy in stores; and at one time the government *forced* the marketplaces into the towns, sparing only a few like Fonds-des-Nègres (Mintz 1960a).[33] This marketplace welcomed 15,000 buyers and sellers or more on a brisk Tuesday; at Fonds-des-Nègres, with only one store as an exception, it is the storekeepers who must travel, coming from the towns to sell in the market. As a result, rural buyers get a marginally better deal.

I had already gotten to know someone from that district and learned about Mme. Anaïs Adrien, a businesswoman or *kòmèsâ* there.[34] Her hamlet, Duverget, a collection of scattered homesteads and fields, was about a two-mile, gently uphill walk from the marketplace. Nana was among dozens of women marketers whom I got to know who lived around Fonds-des-Nègres. I was in Haiti not to study a local community but to learn about the marketers within the system. Yet I had already learned in Jamaica that it is feckless to study market women in the marketplace if one does not know them already. They are simply too busy most of the time to be bothered by some silly foreigner's questions. I got to know Nana first, and then she introduced me to her friends and taught me an enormous amount about marketing and also about her own life.

When we first became friends—her son, Jis (Gustave), had already helped me greatly with my initial work in Fonds-des-Nègres—she was in her late fifties, a plump, silent woman deeply intent on her

Nana Adrien (seated) and her son, Gustave. Behind Nana stands
Gustave's sister, Eria. Milouze, Eria's daughter, stands next to Nana.
Habitation Duverger, Fonds-des-Nègres, Haiti, 1959.

business ventures. Every two weeks she made a round trip from her village to the capital, Port-au-Prince, buying and selling. At first I thought Nana really had no other interests but her children and her business. When one of my students, whom I was able to help to settle in her village, told me some months later that she was a serious, enthusiastic, and generous supporter of vodoun, I was genuinely surprised. In my company she was mostly silent, even shy, until my interest in her work awakened her own.

Nana was born in 1902 and had been going to market since her infancy. Her first business dealing was in sugar; her mother gave her 1 centime to buy a packet of sugar, which she resold for 2 centimes on returning home. She explained to me that the centime she earned was *bénéfis* (profit) whereas the centime she had been given was not *lajâ* but *mâmâlajâ*—that is, not money, but capital. Nana's mother traveled regularly to Port-au-Prince before the American occupation in 1915, and occasionally Nana would be taken along—four days' travel by mule each way. Though the U.S. occupation was much deplored, and justly, both by North American critics and by the Haitian bourgeoisie, Nana remembered it mostly because it provided people in her region with an easier way to get to the capital to buy and sell. Thereafter, over her lifetime, Nana learned how to negotiate and haggle, how to judge quality, how to cipher, how to measure— like most Haitian market women, Nana was illiterate—and how to cope with the many perils of market trade.

She had raised five children, mostly by herself—her husband had died in 1939, when the youngest was only two years old—hiring labor to work her land and getting most of her income from marketing. Though she had begun as a local *révâdèz* at Fond-des-Nègres, by the time I knew her she had been doing much more serious and demanding work for nine years. Her income was very substantial by Haitian rural standards; she was grossing as much as US$400.00 monthly. Every other Friday she carried produce she had purchased during the weekly market in the neighboring town of l'Asile and around her own rural section *(sèksyô)* to Port-au-Prince, by truck. Depending on availability and season, she sold husked and un-husked sorghum *(pitimi)*, ginger, peanuts, pumpkins, fowl, and eggs. She would stay in Port-au-Prince till Monday morning, selling and sleeping on sacks of grain in the depot—then buying goods to carry back to her home village.

It is difficult to imagine the difficulties and danger with which each such trip confronts the intermediaries. Most of the food they carry is highly perishable. Trucks often go off the road, even fall into ravines—people can die of injuries. For most of rural Haiti, there was no—*no*—medical care of any sort. I remember one particularly taxing trip to the Cap Haïtien regional hospital in a raging thunderstorm down a dark mountain road, carrying a local peasant (badly gored by a bull) and four members of his family. It was a distance of about thirty miles. There is no doubt at all that he would have died if I had not been there to give him a ride.

In the trade itself, dealers cheat; patrons go back on their word; there are thieves, some of them very clever. Capital is extremely hard to come by. Countless women start marketing, only to fail. Most of us would fail, too. The competition is stiff, the dangers many (Mintz 1964). Yet Nana pursued her profession with zeal and sometimes even with pleasure, each round trip a measure of her skill and success.

In order to understand better her mode of operation, I might carry her and her stock to Port-au-Prince in my Land Rover. It was then an enjoyable trip, I thought—fewer than a hundred miles, but nearly six hours over difficult terrain—with one gas station and six Duvalier guard posts en route. The guards often could not read. They were armed with either ancient Lee Enfield rifles or Thompson submachine guns. They always seemed at least as scared as I was. My anxiety was, as they say, reality based.

When the rivers were high, it might easily have become a two-day trip—though we never got stuck. Nana carried bread, bananas, water, and *clairin* (Cr. *klérê*), the raw local rum, for her own nourishment on every trip. On reaching the city, I would take her to her regular depot *(magazê)*, watch the unloading of her stock while she greeted her friends there, and set the time for our return trip on Monday. I visited her each day in the depot for several hours to watch her transactions. When I would leave her at night, I would drive through the market area to my *pension*. I was familiar enough to the police there to be left alone, in spite of Duvalier. The sidewalks, along the market streets, some of them arcaded, were always lined at midnight with hundreds of sleeping women from all over the nation, each on her own burlap sack.

Monday morning we would load up three five-gallon tins of lard, twenty-five gallons of *clairin,* some yards of blue denim, two boxes of locally made soap, and a few items to satisfy special requests. Locally made white and yellow soap *(savô blâ, savô djô)* for bath and laundry was one of the Haitian peasants' true necessities, and the demand for soap was inelastic. The Duvalier regime's tax increases on soap was among its nastier everyday exactions.

Richer than most marketers, Nana was able to leave some of her less perishable stock at the depot to be sold by associates or the depot owner on commission during the week, when prices often rose.

Nana and friends, market warehouse,
Port-au-Prince, Haiti, 1959.

Women with less capital could not hold back that way. Nor could poorer women enjoy the luxury of sleeping, safe and dry, in a depot. We would get back to Fonds-des-Nègres that afternoon and deposit the stock in the house of a *komè (commère)* on the road, from which it would be moved by burro *(bourik)* to Nana's house in Duverget the following day.[35]

It was always a pleasure to be reminded just how smart Nana was, sharpened by her lifetime in the market. I might ask her about local marketing by choosing a hypothetical situation of a classic sort. For example, one quickly learns in a Haitian market that sellers of the same item gather in the same place, and that the same item always *seems* to sell at the same asking price. What would she do, I recall asking, if she and several friends were selling red beans at 3.5 gourdes the *gro mamit,* and a new marketer appeared who was willing to sell at 3 gourdes? She cocked her head and chuckled, asking me a question that immediately laid bare the intimate link between theory and practice. "How many *pwa rouj* does she have?" "Oh," I said, about a dozen *gro mamit.*" "Oh, we would let her sell," she said simply. "And what if she had a whole lot?" "Ah, then we would aim to buy her out!" Nana knew about oligopsony, all right; as well as about capital, long-term supply costs, zero opportunity costs, marginal utility, and arbitrage—but she and her sisters had no need of Western terminology.

Of course, sometimes not even experience, intelligence, and courage are enough. When money is scarce in Port-au-Prince and the local supply of food piles up, skill and even daring cannot change the situation. The taxes that *machâ* paid were always extortionate. And there are other catastrophes besides gluts and taxes, such as political violence or war. In 1957 while she slept in a Port-au-Prince *dépo,*

Market day at Fonds-des-Nègres market, Haiti.

Nana was robbed of nearly a thousand gourdes—US$200. She almost gave up her trips then, she told me.[36]

In my work with market women, I discovered significant similarities to some of the economic maneuvers reported for West African marketers by anthropologists and economists who had worked there. In societies where capital is rare and labor cheap, people engage in near-superhuman feats to get their hands on operating capital, and informal interest rates can be astronomical. Haitian market women were willing to pay interest for three days' use of capital that would have amounted to 600 percent if it were calculated on an annual basis. It was while working with Nana and her friends that I first recognized that extortionate rates of interest on even the most modest of loans was a major obstacle to economic growth in such societies.

The West African practice of "Gold Coasting," which requires the swift sale of goods at an extremely low rate of profit so that the supplier can be paid off in as little as seventy-two hours (Bauer 1954:22–34), was common in large Haitian markets. Such transoceanic similarities argue for a common cultural heritage. But in at least some cases, it may be structurally parallel economic situations producing like solutions rather than a shared tradition.

The contributions people like Nana make to their society are enormous. Thousands of industrious and daring Haitians, many of them grandmothers, match the output of their husbands and sons, support scores of trucks, feed the cities, sustain the agricultural countryside, educate their children (who receive no education other than at high cost). It is these unlettered peasants who have made the internal market system the vibrant institution it has been for more than two hundred years.

In their marketing, Haiti's women are economically independent of their families. No Haitian husband would dream of asking his wife to use her capital for any expense he incurs. All Haitian husbands take great pride in the marketing skills of their wives. Marketing by women, that is, constitutes a nearly perfect opposition to the agricultural labor of men; and the attitudes of men and women about their economic labors are more modern than (let us say) those of many of us middle-class Americans. A woman's success never shames her husband. This seeming "modernity" is based on old values that go back, I am sure, at least to slavery times, some of them possibly to Africa itself (Mintz 1971b, 1975).

Tom Belnavis in Jamaica and Nana Adrien in Haiti, both of them now gone, represent for me the achievements and tragedy of Caribbean peasant life. In the aftermath of slavery, the ancestors of such people, showing enormous energy and determination, built new ways of life for themselves, ways of seeing and doing that drew on their pasts but were constructed, bit by bit, out of their ongoing lives. The peasants' aspirations were frustrated in both societies. In Jamaica, planter ideology was wedded to racism and contempt for the peasantry. In Haiti, where a peasantry flourished, the ruling elite lived on peasant sweat. People like Nana, instead of being helped to build their businesses, were encumbered by taxation and lacked an infrastructure to provide reasonable business loans, schools for their children, roads, buses, decent market roofs and stands, and clean toilets—services that the taxes exacted from them each day could have paid for. In Jamaica, the peasantry declines with each passing day. In Haiti, the peasantry is dying now.

The profoundest drama of the Caribbean region, I think, lies in its rootedness in a violent and degraded past. That is because it stands to this day as a testament to the courage and creativity of those millions who were dragged from their hearths, mostly to awful suffering, humiliation, and early deaths, in what may have been the single most terrible demographic event in history. The Jamaican and Haitian people are their descendants. I believe that knowing something of the ways that Nana Adrien and those thousands of others like her talked and worked and lived helps us to better understand that past.

4

Puerto Rico

MY THIRD ANCIENT COLONY, politically, is perhaps the region's most ancient colony of all. Puerto Rico differs greatly from both Jamaica and Haiti. The three societies share much the same climate, flora, and fauna and in broad outlines a good deal of their social history. Yet each is distinctive, yielding considerable contrastive insight when examined in detail. It seems to me that Puerto Rico, when looked at comparatively, may be the most illuminating.

For more than a century after 1492, the Caribbean remained a Spanish sea. The four big islands—the three of concern to me here and Cuba—stayed entirely Spanish for a century and a half after their conquest. Though by the 1620s Spain's European rivals had begun to claim and colonize the lesser islands, all four big islands remained Spanish. As we have seen, among the larger islands Jamaica was the first prize to fall to northern Europe, wrested from Spain by Britain in 1655—163 years after Columbus. Santo Domingo, larger than any other Antillean island but Cuba, remained wholly Spanish until almost the start of the eighteenth century. But foreigners, mainly French, had hunted, raided, smuggled, and traded in the western third of that island, in defiance of Spanish rule, long before then. What became French Saint Domingue was not officially ceded to France until 1697, 205 years after the Discovery. Then in 1804, French Saint Domingue was reborn as the Republic of Haiti. Puerto Rico, however, stayed Spanish (as did Cuba) until 1898–99. After the North American seizure, Cuba would be given nominal independence. But Puerto Rico, a Spanish colony for not quite a decade less than four full centuries, was not. It became an American dependency and has remained that ever since.

After 1655, Jamaica went on to become Britain's most profitable island colony. And fewer than fifty years later, Saint Domingue became France's colonial golden goose. Both colonies were thrust on the same awful path to economic success by their European masters. Both when at their most lucrative were at their most destructive in human terms.

The history of Puerto Rico was markedly different from these other two societies. For one thing, unlike them, Puerto Rico is both a new colony and an old one. First settled by Spain in 1508, Puerto Rico became a prize of war in 1898. Though it has since experienced several transitions, it remains firmly attached to the United States. Its people are United States citizens, though they cannot exercise all of a citizen's rights when living in Puerto Rico itself.

Puerto Rican essayist Tomás Blanco long ago referred to Puerto Rico's political status as a "permanent interim" (interinato permanente). That interim has complicated roots, some less concerned with Puerto Rico than with her colonial master. The United States has never adjusted gracefully to managing the lands and lives of other peoples. Though clearly unwilling to play in public the imperial role many European powers have willingly played in their history, this country has proved adept instead at something that has been referred to—not altogether facetiously—as hitchhiking imperialism. It is clearly not that the United States dislikes having and using power. But apparently it has no appetite for acknowledging in a public, hence more responsible, way the contradictions implicit in frankly colonial rule. Something in our own history makes the idea of our ruling other peoples very difficult to deal with. Puerto Rico's political status certainly has evolved in its century inside the North American "family." But the interim of which Blanco wrote still has not ended. Even today, that status is ambiguous. Puerto Ricans are citizens of the United States. But they experience their citizenship—economically, politically, even culturally—in ambiguous ways; and most North Americans do not even know in what regard the rights of these fellow citizens are compromised.

Though I did my first Caribbean fieldwork in Puerto Rico, in this book I turn to it last. It is the Caribbean country I think I know best, and the one I got to know first. Its history and people impressed me deeply when I first went there. It was because of my experiences there that I became a Caribbeanist. But I did not begin to think analytically about the differences among these island societies until after I had read about, and done fieldwork in, other Caribbean places as well. After Puerto Rico, I had my own (albeit dim and imperfect) Antillean lens with which I often found myself looking at other societies. I think it makes sense to consider this ancient colony last, because its history illuminates for me a profound cultural and sociological division in Caribbean history.

To chart Puerto Rico's distinctive historical path, I turn yet again to sugar, slavery, and the plantation. I hope to show they have had different meanings here. We have noted how, from quite early on, Britain, France, and the Netherlands were eager to plunge into the slave-and-sugar business. The story had been a different one for

Spain. To be sure, Spain introduced sugar, slaves, and the plantation system to the Antilles before anyone else. In Santo Domingo, Spanish colonists made the New World's first sugar in 1511 (Rodríguez Morel 2004), more than a century before any other European power was able even to validate by effective occupation any claim to a speck of land in the islands.

Yet it was not till 250 years later that the Spanish state made a sustained official effort to support its colonial sugar industries. Spain's inability to do so had the effect of keeping Puerto Rico more like Cuba and Santo Domingo, her other remaining Caribbean possessions, rather than like British Jamaica and French Saint Domingue.[1] Puerto Rican composer Rafael Hernández once called Spain's three island colonies "las tres hermanitas," the three little sisters, in a song full of Hispanophile nostalgia. But Spain's economic policy in all three was authoritarian during initial centuries and then became negligent or actively discouraging—often both at once. In the early decades these islands could not fulfill the hopes either of their discoverer or of their royal majesties—and certainly not those Columbus's optimism first inspired in court.

Beginning early in the sixteenth century, the discovery and conquest of highland Mexico and later of the Andes—with their vast populations, sophisticated political systems, and great mineral riches—served further to deepen the lack of royal interest in the islands. The wealth of the mainland, by helping to reduce the tiny settler populations of the Caribbean early in the conquest, helped to turn the first Hispanic colonies into mere fueling stations and oceanic guard posts. Their decline was further hastened in the sixteenth century by the exhaustion of their mineral wealth and the annihilation of their aboriginal peoples.

In his magisterial study of the British and Spanish New World empires, Elliott writes the following about Spain in the Caribbean:

> In principle, the Spanish Caribbean islands—Hispaniola, Cuba, Puerto Rico and Jamaica—might have seemed to offer the same potential in the sixteenth century for the development of mono-cultures based on slave labour as that which was to be realized in the British island of Barbados in the seventeenth century, or indeed in Spain's own possession of Cuba in the later eighteenth. But, after the early years of plunder and ruthless exploitation were over, the Spanish Caribbean became something of an economic backwater. The more ambitious settlers moved on in search of richer prizes on the mainland, and with their departure the white population of the islands stagnated or declined. (2006:105)

These background facts set the scene. But northern Europe's frantic development of sugar plantations in the Caribbean region after 1650 has tended to hide from view the earlier era of uneven Hispanic colonization and rule on the big islands. During the first 125 years, even though sugar plantations were established and enslaved Africans were producing sugar in the "three little sisters," the momentum of expansion soon passed to Spain's rivals, once they successfully seized and held land, first in the smaller islands such as Barbados and eventually in the bigger ones like Jamaica.

The Spanish colonists who enriched themselves by gold mining in Santo Domingo, Cuba, and Puerto Rico before the seventeenth century soon found they had run out of gold; the indigenous Taino people, enslaved to work the mines, were decimated by war, disease, and exhaustion. There had to be some source of wealth beyond metal with which the colonists who remained on the big islands could sustain themselves. But by 1520 Spain, thrilled by the promise of the wealth of *tierra firma*, did little to help the island colonies grow. Royal dislike for private enterprise—whether in plantations or in commerce—came in part from fear that New World colonists who achieved economic success in agriculture and trade would defy the political authority of the metropolis.

Elliott (2006:137) mentions the Crown's "deep suspicion of creole aspirations." Though he refers here particularly to the reluctance to appoint those born in the New World to administrative posts, the suspicion of creoles was even broader. At the same time, the vast flow of metallic treasure from the mainland to Spain had a crushing effect on Spanish industry at home and did not encourage economic experimentation beyond mining overseas. More broadly, the scale of Spanish conquest in the New World was so huge that control and administration were chronically difficult for the metropolis. Though Spain led Europe by carving out colonies in the New World early in the sixteenth century, she seems to have been least able to integrate her colonies with the metropolis itself. An obsession with mineral wealth, the burden of fierce religious conviction, and restrictive rules of trade and of civil governance all typified Hispanic imperial policy, obstructing the growth of a genuinely capitalistic economy that might have better integrated colonies and "mother country."

Religious orders and a few enterprising individuals tried to build a sugar industry in all of the Hispanic colonies (including Jamaica, until it was taken from Spain). But before the eighteenth century, the sugar industry failed to prosper for long anywhere in the Spanish islands.[2] What happened with Hispanic sugar, then, was entirely different from its fate in the British, Dutch, French, and other islands, and the long-term results of those differences cut deeply into the social history of the Hispanic Caribbean.

The reliance on African slave labor in the European settlement of the tropical New World until well into the nineteenth century meant that demography tended to follow the plantation. The number of slaves on the islands of Spain's rivals grew rapidly during the sugar era, while the European settlers remained tiny minorities. But until nearly the nineteenth century, the numbers of slaves in Spain's own islands remained modest. In Puerto Rico, Kinsbruner (1996:2) writes, "economic performance was chronically languid" until a new sugar industry was reestablished in the 1770s.

It was not until then that private property in land in Puerto Rico was actually ordained by the metropolis. This is a striking fact, if we recall that sugarcane had been first planted there early in the sixteenth century to produce sugar for export. The history of the sugar industry itself in Puerto Rico was demonstrably uneven, reflecting the larger uncertainties (Picó 2006:52–56). Though sugar production had risen to 450,000 pounds by 1582, by 1602 it had fallen again to 25,000 pounds. It would rise—and fall—again in that century. The island's role in world sugar production remained slight, before the important expansion that began early in the nineteenth century. In comparison to that of the French or British colonies, Puerto Rico's production would look quite modest even later—indeed, until the North American occupation in the twentieth century.[3]

Rates of slave importation, poorly reported for Puerto Rico, suggest something about the sugar industry there. In 1776, there were only an estimated 5,000 slaves on the island. Even in the 1840s, by which time a solid sugar industry was in place, the number peaked at less than 54,000. At no time in Puerto Rico's history did the slaves reach 12 percent of the total population (Baralt 2007:58). The contrast with the "real" sugar islands is striking. Except for perhaps the first decade or two of settlement, slave numbers in Puerto Rico probably never exceeded the number of free nonwhites.

These sketchy data provide evidence that the social and economic history of Puerto Rico deviated sharply from that of Jamaica and Haiti, beginning at an early time. The Hispanic islands, particularly Puerto Rico and Cuba, while they eventually repeated the sugar-and-slavery experience of the northern European colonies, did so much later in time and under very different conditions. What colonial Puerto Rico had become, socially and economically, before the nineteenth century was as much the result of the absence of plantation development as of anything else.

When one compares population growth in the "sugar islands," British Jamaica and French Saint Domingue, where the labor demands of the plantations led to the arrival of masses of chained Africans and a trickle of Europeans to manage them, neither group reproducing itself, with what happened in Puerto Rico, the revealed differences are quite sharp. In Puerto Rico, the number of free people of African origin grew during the first two centuries and the number of slaves was never large, before the nineteenth century. And from the beginning of settlement until the dawn of the eighteenth century, the rise in the number of physically mixed people on the island must have been continuous.

To appreciate what probably happened, we need to recall again that slaves are a form of capital but an inelastic form of investment. They must be fed, clothed, and housed; they can fall ill and die—and all this, even if their owners have no gainful way to exploit them. The irregular, uneven economic development of Puerto Rico during its first centuries no doubt led to the freeing of slaves whenever the enterprise for which they had been purchased failed or when there was no way to benefit from their labor. A cumulative consequence would be the swift growth of the physically mixed population (anyone with visible phenotypic traits of nonwhite ancestry), at least until the 1840s.[4] Though there are few data to consult on the trade, most scholars believe that slave importations to Puerto Rico before 1800 were small, as well as irregular.[5]

From 1800 until the 1840s, slave importations mounted, and by 1800, immigration from Europe (especially but not only from Spain) was growing. After 1840, even the illegal slave trade declined, while the proportion of whites rose (Picó 2006:187). This does not mean that any of the earlier population elements—Europeans, Native Americans, Africans, and their descendants—had vanished altogether, but they had surely intermixed. Picó's astute history (143) refers to those foreign visitors of the seventeenth and eighteenth centuries who "observed the brown and black appearance of the Puerto Rican population, the result of relationships between the population of European and African origin."

What we see here throws events in the northern European island colonies into stark contrast. In both Jamaica and Saint Domingue, seizure from Spain meant a terrible quickening of the slave plantation economy and an "Africanization" of the population. Meanwhile, Puerto Rico, which received few settlers at first, actually lost population to the mainland in the 1520s. Its "lack of development" really meant simply very slow growth of the island population and considerable isolation from the metropolis. During one eleven-year period, not a single Spanish ship visited the island. Given these circumstances, it is not surprising that smuggling and contraband trade became a way of life for many, while the costs of colonial administration had to be met by the *situado,* funds for the costs of governance, sent regularly from Mexico.

What we know for sure about Puerto Rican rural life in the sixteenth and seventeenth centuries is meager. After the first phase of gold mining, the near disappearance of the native peoples, and sugar's early but limited career, the settlers of Puerto Rico had no choice but to grow their own food and produce and trade what they could.[6] Famine, not slave revolt, was the main threat. Subsistence farming became widespread, often mixed with the cultivation of smallholdings in exportable foods. There was much cattle ranching, as in Cuba, and considerable trade (including smuggling) in leather hides and ginger. Local forestry products, including timber and essential oils for furniture and medicinal uses, were exported. The New World's vast floral wealth and its treasure of domesticated plants, coming first from the islands, was now reaching Spain and then spreading elsewhere.

In spite of these rural activities, Puerto Rico's colonial government had to cope with large interior areas, some barely occupied or policed, and those conditions persisted well into the seventeenth century. Scarano writes: "From about 1650 onward, and for a span of more than a century, the rural population outside the walled city of San Juan—now an important military outpost—led a nearly autarchic existence. Though very little is known about the economic history of the period, it is clear that relative isolation from the international economy fostered the growth of an independent, racially mixed peasantry whose contact with the outside world was limited to occasional contraband trade with foreigners" (1984:iv). Not everyone agrees on the extent of such isolation from the outside world, in view of the apparently lively trade; or the idea of a walled city cut off from its hinterland. I am not sure that the term "peasantry" is exactly right here.[7] Yet Scarano makes clear how strikingly this island's history differed from those of British Jamaica and French Saint Domingue. For a lengthy time, except for the capital and a few small towns and villages, Puerto Rico was a thinly peopled colony marked by only faint and sporadic attempts at change. It had grown slowly for two centuries. "By 1700," Picó writes, "the number of known inhabitants of the island was around 6,000" (2006:96).

This picture of a sparsely occupied and meager rural life is probably accurate for a period stretching from the failures of early settlement and the destruction of the indigenous cultures, almost to the end of the seventeenth century. Interior settlement by squatters, buccaneers, runaway slaves, army and navy deserters—by anyone seeking to escape state regulation—was apparently commonplace. Picó, describing Puerto Rico as it was then (and even as late as the 1830s), says: "It was easier to go [from San Juan] to Ponce [on the south coast] by schooner than on horseback. Between Utuado and Arecibo [large towns for their time, in the northwest] one had to wade through the Río Grande de Arecibo 23 times. . . . The majority of the island's inhabitants never got to see the capital city during their lifetime" (2006:177). Yet travel by sea (including smuggling to and from other islands) was lively. Illicit trade with the Virgin and Leeward Islands and with western Santo Domingo (until 1697) was common. And at the same time, we learn from the rare early visitors to the island about the strange, "indolent" island dwellers who lived—almost free of governance, some said—in the highlands, over

the course of more than two centuries. There are documented reports of runaway slaves among them, many who had come from
other islands. Puerto Rico's free population in the seventeenth and
eighteenth centuries included persons of complex ancestry: a genetic inheritance of Spanish colonists, Taino and other Indians, and
Africans, both slave and free—whose governance, some students
have argued, was virtually null.[8]

Because of this demographic history, Puerto Rican society differs
from those of Jamaica and Saint Domingue at comparable historical
moments. When the Puerto Rican plantation economy began to
grow rapidly again after 1800, it had to deal with different challenges. In Jamaica and Saint Domingue, where sparse numbers of
Europeans had rapidly introduced enormous populations of enslaved Africans, the results were social systems structurally similar
to each other but similarly different from Puerto Rico—different
proportions of free and slave, of white and black, and of people of
color, living in the Puerto Rican case without the almost military am-
bience typical of Caribbean plantation societies. Both economically
and socially and in spite of the early introduction of slavery to
Puerto Rico, I believe that the societies in which slavery became the
principal basis of the economy, such as Jamaica and Saint Domingue,
were qualitatively different.

When in the nineteenth century Puerto Rico began to repeat the
seventeenth-century plantation experiences of Jamaica and French
Saint Domingue, several conditions made the Puerto Rican case different from those others. The rising class of planters in Puerto Rico
undertook energetically to use slaves as their labor force, but it was
not easy. The growing unpopularity of slavery in Europe—Britain
outlawed the trade in 1809, then bullied Spain into a treaty promis-

ing to do the same in 1820—made obtaining slaves more and more difficult. Another difference between Puerto Rico and the classic Caribbean plantation colonies arose from Puerto Rico's meager and uneven economy in the sixteenth and seventeenth centuries. Boom and bust made the freeing of slaves a common practice, and was one of the forces that had led during those centuries to the settlement of the island's interior. By 1800, the Puerto Rican highlands were home to a scattered population of free and racially mixed people, most of them squatter farmers. Poorly clad, laconic, hospitable and peaceful, these were the people who gave rise to that highly romanticized rustic figure of Puerto Rican literature, the jíbaro.

But they inhabited a society where there were few slaves. Soon there would be no more slaves to be had legally, and only few who could be smuggled in successfully. It may have been inevitable that someone would think of finding a way to put those free squatters— of any color—to work on the plantations alongside or in place of slaves; and of course someone did.

In the whole of Caribbean history, only in Puerto Rico did the local planters undertake to solve their labor problem (with metropolitan help, of course) by impressing their own poor and free (and in some cases white) landless people.[9] This "solution" is of interest, among other things, because it seems to have oppressed all of the poor, of whatever color, equally. By legal definition, the landless rural dwellers were transformed into "idlers" *(vagos)*. A prescribed number of days worked each year on the plantations were designated to rescue them from idleness. This was first specified by law in 1824. After 1827, the laws became more severe. The landless and the squatters—*agregados* and *desacomodados*—had to carry workbooks that recorded the days worked and for which plantation. By

1835, Puerto Rico had 40,875 *agregados*, and 34,336 slaves (Mintz 1951; Turnbull 1840).[10] Not until 1873 were the labor laws for landless Puerto Ricans abolished, at the same time as slavery.

The half century during which free and enslaved people worked and lived side by side in the Puerto Rican countryside undoubtedly affected the evolution of social attitudes about race in that country. Such an experience may have done little or nothing to eliminate racism. But it changed, and may have complicated, the way Puerto Ricans saw themselves and saw others; it probably influenced their opinions of rural labor; and it may have affected what they came to think differences in "race" meant.[11] I suspect that neither color nor plantation labor ever carried so heavy a stigma in Puerto Rico as in Jamaica—at least partly because plantation laborers in Puerto Rico have always been of diverse cultural and racial origins.[12]

Puerto Rico also differed from my other two ancient colonies because the staggering majorities of people of African origins and phenotype, typical of Jamaica and Saint Domingue, never developed in the Puerto Rican case. The perpetuation of African cultural materials—though certainly commoner than the Puerto Rican intelligentsia ever acknowledged—was always weaker there than in the other two cases.[13]

The Hispanic Caribbean generally fails to perceive African-American cultures and peoples in the manner of the French or British Caribbean. Yet the ways people perceive and think of particular cultural items—such as speech, or language, or dance—are powerful factors in whether and how they may be manifested, and then in the interpretations made of their manifestation. Societies that deal differently with such cultural expressions usually deal differently with "race" as well. In the case of Puerto Rico, even the particular imputed (and wrong) interconnections between race and behavior are in some ways distinctive. I also contend that within the Hispanic Caribbean there are differences as well in the ways that men and women, and the very relations between them, are perceived and acted out. But I will return to these assertions later.

In 1948 I began my fieldwork in Puerto Rico, settling in Jauca, a tiny south coast roadside hamlet, named after the district (barrio) within which it lay. A hundred yards east along the road stood a crumbling square brick chimney, all that was left of one of the extinct sugar mills, with whose ruins the south coast was dotted.[14] There were a few little stores and a dozen modest houses farther along the road; another twenty houses or so on a patch of parched earth, stretching toward the bay about an eighth of a mile away; and other roadside houses, closer to town. Nearly everybody in the village worked in the sugarcane at that time.

I lived in a small one-room shack divided in two by a wood partition; Santos, a young cane cutter, occupied the other half. His sister Pola made me my dinners. Each meal arrived at dusk in an enameled metal lunchbox called a *fiambrera,* consisting of three tiered pots: rice and red beans, boiled tubers such as sweet potatoes and yams, occasionally a piece of sausage, or rarely, a fish soup. If I were out late talking or drinking or fishing, the food would sit inside my door next to a dimly lighted kerosene lamp until I got home, famished. I would eat in the near-dark so as not to disturb Santos, since he always arose at dawn. Pola's little daughters washed and ironed my clothes and served me my morning coffee or chocolate in a polished coconut cup. Often they brought me a ripe papaya, the dew still clinging to it. Evenings I was able at times to feast on tiny, delicious oysters that grew on the nearby mangroves. No one else would eat them, but children would gather them, simply for the treat of watching *el americano* eat them and wash them down with *un shirli* (from Shirley Temple)—a half-pint of the local rum.

I was treated kindly by everyone—though one could see, too, that I was regarded with faint embarrassment because in many ways I was so obviously a total idiot. I stayed in that village—slept in that shack, ate that food, in a state bordering on perfect bliss—for a year and a half.

One of the persons I got to know when I settled in Barrio Jauca,now more than sixty years ago, was Dn. Tomás Famanía, a tough, wiry old man who still worked in the cane. Because he was so fit and sturdy, he was known locally as *el guayacán,* the name of the tree having beautiful, iron-hard, yellow-and-brown wood that we call lignum vitae, from which moving parts for machines were once made and from which more recently cutting boards, plates, and mortars and pestles were fashioned. Famanía endeared himself to me especially because of his habit of dancing with little girls at public dances in the barrio. Families came to the dances. I found the sight of that skinny, ragged old man, then in his sixties, doing the bolero with a six-year-old, profoundly charming. The little girls were always charmed, too, and *el guayacán* unfailingly courtly.

Famanía was also a talker. He reminisced, for example, about the arrival of the Americans. He was a youngster himself at that time. The day the American soldiers appeared, his mother had sent him to collect tinder in *el monte*—patches of scrub vegetation growing a thousand yards inland—and while he was doing so, he heard drumming in the distance, along the road where he lived. He ran all the way back, in time to see *los soldados norteamericanos* marching eastward from Ponce to Salinas and passing through the roadside hamlet of Jauca. Because he'd come back with no firewood, he got whipped, too. Tomás had a wry sense of humor. "First came the Americans" (1898), "and then San Ciriaco" (the 1899 hurricane), he would say. When the Americans built the Ponce and Guayama Railroad along that road, they cut down all of the rare tropical hardwoods that grew in *el monte*—the *caoba* and *guayacán, tabonuco* and *úcar* and *frescura*—and made railroad ties of them.

That was the part of the Puerto Rican past that I came to know best—the one that followed directly on the North American conquest, when a new stage of the plantation economy unfolded on the south coast of the island. I was wrong to think that the Americans had completely remade the technology of sugar production; a couple of modern factory centrals were working before their arrival. But I was not wrong about the new scale of operations, or about the changes in human relations in economic life that unfolded. Before 1898, there had been the sugar haciendas—family-owned estates with their complements of resident labor, growing cane—sometime after the start of the nineteenth century, such as the Hacienda Dn. Pastor Díaz, the ruins of which remained in Jauca. In my work I was not able to establish exactly when this hacienda began working, but the local industry reached a peak in the 1840s and 1850s and then declined. The Americans arrived half a century later, with sugar entrepreneurs among them who had ambitious plans for this new colony.[15] In the first decades of the twentieth century, large upland stretches adjacent to the alluvial flood plains of the coast were cleared of scrub vegetation and tropical woods to be made into pastures for herds of oxen that would be used to haul cane. The flood plains themselves, with their hacienda ruins, were soon bought up or leased by the Americans at excellent prices and consolidated into vast landholding corporations.

A system of irrigation, much of it subsidized with government money, was created to water the emerging megaplantations. The island's south coast had too little natural rainfall for an optimum sugarcane crop. Irrigation is better than rain, if there is a choice; it can easily be increased or reduced. The numerous little pre-1900 haciendas were soon supplanted by gigantic central factories; south coast production enjoyed staggering increases.

One day there would arrive sugar's famed "Dance of the Millions," when world sugar prices ballooned crazily. A few years later, in October 1929, came the global economic collapse. But while the system was still expanding, the southern littoral of Puerto Rico quickly became an ocean of sugarcane, almost from one end of the island to the other. The old haciendas had individual names— Hacienda Alomar, Hacienda Capó, Hacienda Pastor Díaz, and so on. Even the poorest local people knew all of the owners by sight. Now, however, haciendas morphed into *colonias*—defined as landholdings only, without mills: tiny integers in a mosaic of thousands of corporately managed acres. Each *colonia* had its *mayordomo* and its small cluster of resident peons. The old hacienda machinery was shipped away to Japan or some other place or left to rust. A Department of Commerce report of 1917 notes that on the land now cultivated by one of the largest U.S. corporations, thirty-one old hacienda mills had once ground cane (U.S. Department of Commerce 1917:248). Now all of the cane in the same area could be ground by a single mill.

Along with this big change in the industry came a movement of impoverished peasants from the highlands to the coasts, fleeing the

Typical *colonia* housing on a sugarcane plantation, southern Puerto Rico.

damage done by the terrible hurricane of San Ciriaco (1899). Poverty and disaster helped solve the labor needs of the burgeoning American plantations. Sugar became largely North American in ownership and management. Engineers, chemists, technicians, accountants, and lawyers came from the United States to keep the corporate plantation system running.

When I was doing my fieldwork, the corporation next to whose lands I lived (Central Aguirre Corp. and its landholding affiliate, Luce y Cía.) had its offices in a nearby town, Guayama.[16] The center of operations was a company town in and of itself, with stores, bars, a small athletic center with a boxing ring, and a baseball diamond. As one drove onto the grounds of the plant one saw the pretty white houses of corporate officialdom, with their green lawns and white fences, the clubhouse, and nearby, the immense grinding mill. On the far side of the mill were the workers' houses, which were numerous and neither pretty nor white. As I did my fieldwork, I visited the plant from time to time; one of the managers had kindly helped me to learn how the land and mills were integrated to maximize efficiency. My dear friend and field assistant, Charlie Rosario, went with me a couple of times, but finally begged off. He said that the white houses with the green lawns and the dark little Puerto Rican girls who were the nannies for the blonde little corporate babies "wore him out." That did not exactly describe what he meant. Charlie's mother was North American; but when Charlie was in Aguirre, he completely forgot that side of his ancestry. I could see why.

All of that is gone now—indeed, sugarcane is nearly gone from Puerto Rico. Worldwide, and even in the United States, sugar is less and less a source of the world's sweetness, though the absolute quantities of sucrose from cane and beet worldwide continue to rise. In 1948, I would not have been able to imagine that coast without sugarcane. The cane grew up to the stoops of workers' houses, the fields tilled and watered like a well-tended garden, the ripe cane towering ten or twelve feet above the sharply demarked pathways *(callejones)*. But in recent decades, as the world market is given its shape more and more by technical advance and the exercise of decisive political and military power, swift transformations—from bustling activity to idleness and despair; or from idleness and despair to bustling activity—have come to seem less and less surprising.

In the village where I worked, the family I came to know best was the Zayas family, headed by Dn. Anastacio Zayas Alvarado (Taso), a sugarcane worker, and his companion and later wife, Elí Villarronga. My friend Taso, who was born in 1908, spent much of his childhood at work, standing knee-deep in water, carrying a lantern to light the way for irrigation workers, at the time when the American corporations were clearing land, preparing to install a modern plantation system. As he grew older, Taso became an irrigation ditch digger *(palero)* himself but also worked at nearly every task that cane cultivation required. I came to know him when he was forty; we remained friends until his death in 1996. He witnessed the evolution of the plantation system in that barrio, from the imposition of the North American corporate system on the much smaller family-owned haciendas until its virtual eradication in the 1970s; and he knew every foot of the thousands of *cuerdas* (a *cuerda* is slightly less than an acre) of land around the barrio.

Taso's experiences meshed so neatly with the events that had marked the history of Puerto Rico's sugar industry that one might say his life could almost have been predicted from that history. But

Dn. Taso, Barrio Jauca, Puerto Rico, 1949.

I think it is also the case that regional history there was made much more comprehensible through the story of his life. Having recorded his reminiscences, I will not impose on readers a précis of the book we wrote together (Mintz 1960b, 1989) but will retell instead one incident, for what it offers about the man and his family during their hardest years.

The year was 1932—a time of unspeakable poverty for the Puerto Rican people. Work in the sugarcane, if there was any work at all, paid very badly. Taso explained that they were working a twelve-hour day, 6 a.m. to 6 p.m., and that his take-home pay for a week of work was US$5.80. He was in his young manhood, living with Elí, and Carmen, their first child. He was working at that time as a *palero,* a ditcher and ditch repairman, the most skilled field laborer.

Taso was a Socialist, in fact a charter member of the Puerto Rican Socialist Party, and sergeant-at-arms of the Comité Roja in the municipality of Sta. Isabel, where Barrio Jauca is. He and his common-law wife Elí voted the Socialist ticket and did not hide their affiliation, in spite of severe and intense repression. One day he was sent to repair a broken canal at a nearby *colonia,* Colonia Texidor. Working alongside him was a man with whose politics Taso disagreed. While they worked, their foreman approached. Taso tells it:

> We were not discussing politics at the moment, but when the *mayordomo,* Dn. Benigno Patiño, arrived, the other one began to show off his politics. And I, never being one to hide his ideals from anyone—I always thought this way—we undertook to discuss politics, he defending his party and I speaking about mine. I was a little partisan about my party; I already had much love

Members of the Zayas Colón family.
Barrio Jauca, Puerto Rico, 1949.

for it. Well, the *mayordomo* did not mix in the conversation. And I remained at work the rest of the day and came home; and when I went to work the next day they told me there was no work. And the next day there was no work; and it soon became clear that work had ended for me. I believe this was the reason for my being suspended from work—the conversation right in front of the *mayordomo,* then the *mayordomo* reacted in that way. I was what you would consider a long time without any work at all. (Mintz 1960b:147)

Elí, Taso's wife, was pregnant at the time, and she remembered the episode well. Elí was characteristically more explicit than Taso about her feelings:

Well, Taso went off to work and came back because they gave him no work. According to what he said, it was an arrogance on the part of that *mayordomo* Patiño, done to him because of politics. We were Socialists at the time and they wanted to punish Taso because he was in politics. They retaliated by not giving him work, and that was when we really began to suffer. He would go out looking for work at all of the *colonias* and wouldn't find any. And Mama would help us out "with a plate," as we say. If it were only water she was boiling at home, she would still send some to me. Many times you would see the plate of food she sent being shared between us two and a small child—it seems to me it was Carmen Iris, because that was when I was pregnant with Pablín. Carmen was already weaned. And we spent a long time that way. That was the period when if we had eight or nine cents, we always used to buy cornmeal, because you got the

Dña. Elí, Barrio Jauca, Puerto Rico, 1949.

most for your money. The way to make it go farthest was to boil it till it was soft. I used to take that cornmeal and put it in a pot of water to boil, and that cornmeal would be spitting around in the pot; I was trying to get the most out of it, and with the cornmeal I painted the kitchen yellow. . . .

During that time I was pregnant with Pablín, and we were in the worst possible condition. I had not been able to prepare even a rag for the birth. The only good dress I had was in the trunk; it was made of a cloth that they call *claro de luna*. And when the moment arrived when I had to make the little shirts for when the child would be born, there was no other way of doing it . . . I took the dress—which I had for an emergency, you see, if it should happen that I had to go to the hospital—I took my new dress and I put it to the scissors and I made, it seems to me, three or four little shirts from the skirt, which was full. And for bonnets, I made several from the top part. I made little bonnets, and those were the bonnets I used on Pablín when he was born.

That *mayordomo* made me angry, you know? I said he was a man without a heart, that he was a man who didn't think of the sufferings of others—he didn't think about how a man's family could go hungry. He didn't think that perhaps some day the same thing might happen to him, to suffer hunger with his children. (Mintz 1960b:149)

Part of the impact of these passages—for me, at least—quite aside from the glimpse into Puerto Rican politics in the 1930s, is how different the lives and outlooks of these wage-earning, clock-conscious, store-dependent people were from the those of the peasant folk with whom I would later work in Jamaica and in Haiti.

The American invasion and occupation of Puerto Rico (1898–99) came very late in the life of Caribbean plantation societies—nearly four centuries after the first sugar produced in the region had been shipped to Spain. In the early history of Puerto Rico, as in eastern Cuba and eastern Santo Domingo, characteristic rural social patterns had developed, and the evolution of these Hispanic Caribbean colonies had deviated from the better known sugar history of other Antillean colonies. But the plantation system, mostly installed in Puerto Rico after 1898, and by the Americans, set the island on a developmental path that would change rural life there. Taso and Elí were not peasants, nor had their parents been. In what I wrote about their village, I described them as rural proletarians. Landless, owning no productive property of any kind, such people had only their labor to sell.

I do not deal here at any length with the contrast between peasants and proletarians in the Caribbean past. The terms have often been used as pure types: mutually complementary and mutually exclusive. Yet in the land history of the islands, they have often been overlapping and conjoint.[17] That shows up in what I have said here. The slaves (slaves of course were really neither "type") who produced their own food and often sold their surpluses in markets; the peasants who went down to coastal plantations during the harvest seasons to earn extra cash; people like Tom Belnavis's wife, Leah, working on the road; Tom himself, cutting cane while maintaining his fields; Taso's wife, Elí, selling candy or tickets in the illegal numbers game to help keep the family fed—such merging activities do not form a third category of rural labor so much as uncover the inadequacy of the other categories.

But though the categories are artificial in describing what people

Cutting line, Colonia Destino, Barrio Jauca,
Santa Isabel, Puerto Rico.

do to live, the contrast they illuminate is real. Even as Caribbean rural people partake of both ways of life in their daily experience, proletarian and peasant life are built around quite different economic subsystems. If peasants and proletarians could be said to mark the two poles of Caribbean rural life, then Tom Belnavis stood at one and Taso Zayas at the other. Many differences between them are functions of the different agrarian histories of the two societies. I do not mean to say that Puerto Rico is a rural proletarian country or Jamaica a peasant country. The rural histories of both places are too complex to be reduced to such simplification. Both of these societies had peasant and rural proletarian populations when I studied them and had had them for a very long time. It is true that the subregion in which Taso lived had not been occupied by a peasantry for at least a century. But before the nineteenth-century sugar boom, the local economy had been quite different; later, when the sugar industry declined, there were real attempts by local workers to establish peasant production.[18] At least since the 1840s, though, the southern coastal plains of Puerto Rico have mostly been the home of sugarcane. In Jamaica, by way of contrast (and even though from the hills of Sturge Town one looks down on the sugarcane fields of Jamaica's north coast), the village itself was by most measures a peasant village. This was true even though some people in it, such as Tom Belnavis, commuted to the coast nearby to work in sugar, while others found work as maids in the houses of the Brown's Town middle classes.

I want to add more here to my impressions of Puerto Rican culture, in three particular regards. One is gender relations, as in the case of Taso and Elí and the people among whom they lived. The second is race relations, as exhibited by the ways people behaved in

Pay line, Colonia Destino, Barrio Jauca,
Santa Isabel, Puerto Rico.

their village and, perhaps more broadly, in Puerto Rico. The last, which I offer even more tentatively, has to do with issues of self and violence. I think that there may be similarities and differences here that throw light on the two other Caribbean societies, as well as on our own.

Several sociological features of the people of Jauca struck me forcibly when I settled there, half a century ago. Though nearly everyone in Jauca was Catholic, no one there went to church;[19] and though all the cohabiting couples there considered themselves married, in fact with only the rarest exceptions, nobody was, by either civil or religious ritual. "Consensual" or common-law unions were at that time the commonest basis for marriage among working-class people. People seemed to manage quite well without either civil or religious blessing.

Though many persons had lived in more than one such union, family life in the barrio was quite stable in regard to child care, relationships to siblings and affines, and most everyday family issues. At that time, nonecumenical churches coming from the United States were proselytizing heavily among local villagers. But the vast majority of local people chose to *identify* themselves as Catholic, even though they did not go to church or to confession, and baptized their children ad libitum. They really did baptize them, but not in church, and without a priest (Mintz and Wolf 1950).

I mention these facts because they did not at first seem to me to fit with the extremely strict chaperonage of female children, among even the very poor, and even in places like Jauca. Indeed, the concern with virginity and the nervous family surveillance over young girls bordered—I thought—on the obsessive. In spite of this surveillance, unions were almost invariably established by elopement, described by the term *llevarse*, to carry off someone *(se la lleva)*. An elopement usually lasted twenty-four hours; it was usually accompanied by sound and fury, particularly on the part of the girl's mother and brothers; in the end, the outrage signified little. In no case known to me did violence occur because of an elopement. Repeatedly, the new couple would establish themselves in a modest shack within forty-eight hours or so, usually aided by the boy's relatives, whereupon shouting for vengeance would come to an end.[20] To separate a young woman from her natal family for twenty-four hours signaled the end of her virginity and established her in a new social category. Whether the families of bride and groom became close afterward depended on several variables, including at what distance the two families lived apart and whether there were any felt differences—in religion or class, say—between them. Often they did draw closer after the birth of the first child. In those days such unions were not followed by a marriage of the couple, either by civil or religious ceremony.

I think there is no doubt that these ways of doing things were learned by the young who grew up in such communities and perpetuated by them through time. I suspect that they were typical of the rural poor, at least in the southern sugarcane zones, for at least a hundred years, if not longer. Such patterns must have developed in spite of the presence of a system of harsh control over the labor of the rural poor, free and slave, black and white; but also in accord with the near-total absence of civil or religious interest in the lives of the same people.[21]

The pattern of fierce chaperonage, elopement, feigned rage, and rapid reconciliation struck me as an important bundle of beliefs and expectations conventionally understood by the participants. But during my time in Jauca I discovered that this "complex," or bundle, of social features fitted neatly with a strikingly different pattern, one of homicide, which was at that time a major local cause of death. Homicides were brought on either by insults real or fictive to masculine identity or by sexual jealousy, which became so mixed up with masculine dignity that it looked almost like the same thing.

One early morning I had crossed the main road in Jauca on an errand when I was suddenly witness to an extraordinary—even terrifying—scene. A young man known to me came running frantically out of the back of a nearby house, closely pursued by another man who looked familiar but whom I did not know personally. I realized the pursuer was carrying a knife. When they had nearly reached me, the attacker closed the gap and struck, falling on his victim, who also fell, crying out faintly (for his mother), voiding his bowels and spilling lots of blood. I can say now, thinking back nearly sixty years, that an event one has never experienced before can be awfully difficult to imagine, and later, even to describe. The killer— for the victim was indeed dead—climbed to his feet shakily. He was perspiring profusely, but his face was a deathly white. His name (in fact *not* his name) was Dolfo. Turning to one of the nearby spectators who, unlike me, was a local person, he said: "I need to be taken to the police station." I recall thinking at the time that the killer clearly had no interest at all in hiding his identity, even from the police; and it brought to mind those many occasions when we see accused criminals hiding their faces from onlookers. *This* man had no such problems, even though he seemed to be in shock. I was soon to meet some others just like him.

In the following twenty-four hours, I tried to find out what, *culturally* speaking, I had witnessed. The facts are simple. The victim, a man of questionable repute locally, had been carrying on with Dolfo's mother. So Dolfo had killed him. But these facts are *too* simple. The woman was a widow, and her new sexual partner a bachelor. No Hamlet here; and there was a thoroughly un-Hamlet context. When I left the scene of the killing and crossed the road, a neighbor asked me what had happened. I mentioned the victim by name—to which my interrogator reacted by asking "Was it Dolfo who did it?" "Yes," I said, very surprised. "Una puñelada?" she responded—the local term for stabbing. "How did you know?" I asked. "He's been carrying it around with him. When I asked him what the knife was for, he said he had to bone a large fish."

And so, did people know ahead of time that Dolfo was going to kill somebody? Was this tragic event "premeditated"? Had anyone else in the barrio ever killed somebody? I learned very quickly that there had been nearly a dozen homicides there in the preceding decade, among a modest population estimated at about six hundred. (*Why had I not known this before?* I berated myself, until I realized that it might have seemed strange indeed to go around that village among my friends asking who the local homicides were, unless that were the purpose of my fieldwork.) I also learned that *all* of those killings had to do with either personal honor or sexual jealousy. At that time in rural Puerto Rico, it was accurate to assert that *that* was why people there killed each other.

In the next municipality—I lived in Santa Isabel, and to our west was a municipality named Juana Díaz—there was a U.S. army airbase. One evening, while talking with friends, I learned that there had recently been two murders near there. It was, I was told, a quite remarkable act of violence. Two male corpses had been dumped from a car onto the shoulder of the road. The victims had been shot. People mulled over this terrible event, and one friend said to me: "This had to be a killing by an American." Have they caught him? I asked. "Oh, no, not so far as I know." But, I persisted, in that case how do you know it was an American? "Tiene que ser un americano. Un puertorriqueño no puede matar así con tanta serenidad." ("It has to be an American. A Puerto Rican can't kill so coolly.") Of course, once having done it, Dolfo was ready to turn himself in. Ready to do so? Once done, possibly even eager to do so. There was no capital punishment in Puerto Rico, and the circumstances being what they were there, a killing like the one I witnessed was *culturally* (not legally) permissible.

I saw something similar once in a neighboring barrio. One morning I left my shack very early because I had to go to San Juan. There were cars *(lineas)* that went from Ponce, to my west, all the way to San Juan, every hour or so, and I was able to flag such a car. This was a big car, already full except for the front seat, where I got in. A mile or two farther, we were hailed very insistently by a young man in a yellow sport shirt and chinos. Though the car was full, the pedestrian signalled so frantically that our driver stopped. There was a conversation—the hopeful passenger indicated he needed a ride only to the nearest town, but urgently. He said without explanation that he was going to the police station there, and he seemed somewhat distraught. The driver let him in, and I sat between him and the driver. There took place a conversation that I would have considered exotic had I heard it before I did fieldwork in Jauca. The driver asked what had happened, and his passenger said a man had been shot at a dance. The driver asked for more information—who shot him—and the man next to me said "I did." Then the driver said, where is the gun, and the passenger said, accidentally poking me with his elbow as he did so, "Right here," and pulled it out of his belt. Then he told the story. He had just arrived from New York the night before, he said, and there was a dance in his barrio. He took his local girlfriend. There was another youth at the dance who insisted on dancing with her. One thing led to another. But of course this fellow had gone to the dance with the gun jammed into his belt. His narrative was spiced with asides, all having to do with his innocence—which is to say, with his declarations to all of us that this act had been forced on him by the ungentlemanly behavior of the victim. When we got to town, he got out, paid his fare, shoved the gun back into his belt, and walked into the police station.

I am reminded of an event that occurred only a year or so later when members of the Puerto Rico Nationalist Party, an armed proindependence political group that rejected the ballot, attacked the Governor's Palace (Fortaleza) in San Juan. Three of the attackers were killed; one guard was seriously wounded. In the subsequent inquiry, the F.B.I. learned that the Fortaleza gardeners came from the penitentiary and some of them were convicted murderers. On learning this, the F.B.I., scandalized, reported their discovery to the governor, Luis Muñoz Marín. His reaction was authentically Puerto Rican: "So what? They aren't mad at *me!*" What I think I had bumped into, in the sphere of personal violence, was a place where people could feel socially compelled to kill; but they killed only because of affronts to their dignity and—as it turned out at that time—*never* for gain.

It would be pretentious to assert that I know either how old or how widespread this moral principle is, and even more so to imagine its origins. But I think of the social history of a society as the garden in which the moral outlooks of a people are cultivated.[22] The largely autonomous lives of these country people—who were free to become and remain culturally homogeneous; who spoke the same language; who lived in small communities and shared a way of life that was given form in the sixteenth century, unencumbered by much external intervention, either religious or civil, at least until the 1800s— might have given birth to that sort of attitude toward violence. This is merely a guess.[23]

I think that, in their attitudes about gender relations, my friends in Jauca conformed quite faithfully to what were broader norms, at least among coastal proletarians. Of course generalities of the sort I offer here are no substitute for a careful analysis of gender differences among Caribbean societies. But I think that some of the differences, as between societies there, show up dramatically. For example, I think that I am right in saying that working-class values in Haiti and Jamaica differed sharply from those that underlay the often homicidal sexual jealousy that seemed to me so common in Jauca. You may remember my picture of rural Haitian market women sleeping in serried rows on the streets of downtown Port-au-Prince during their visits to the capital from their rural districts. If so, and if you have any familiarity with the Hispanic Caribbean, then try to imagine that scene fifty years ago but in Puerto Rico rather than a Haitian or Jamaican setting. If you can do this, you have a much better imagination than I do.

You may also recall my claim that no Haitian peasant could conceive of trying to take from his wife the capital she uses in her market operations. That is a different but not altogether unrelated aspect of Haitian gender norms, which contrasts with those of laboring Puerto Ricans. To make my point, another field anecdote may prove useful.

When I began my fieldwork on Puerto Rico's south coast, many women worked outside the home. But the women I knew who did so were workers' wives, and one way or another they worked in the sugarcane. It was crushingly difficult and unpleasant work—spreading fertilizer, distributing seed, even *jalando pala* (weeding)—but a very few, very poor women did it. They did not, so far as I know, ever cut cane or fill carts *(llenar furgones)*. Those women who did not work outside the home worked inside it. In addition to child care, cleaning, laundry, and cooking, some made candy, or *pasteles,* to sell in the plazas of the *colonias* on payday or on weekends. They would do washing and ironing and needlework—and I mean they *worked.* And when it was enormously popular, as it was in the late 1940s, they sold numbers in the local numbers racket—about which far more could be recounted. In spite of their massive contributions to the stability and survival of the family, women were denied what we would label elementary social freedoms—freedom of movement, for instance—which their husbands enjoyed as a sacred right.

But soon after my first fieldwork in Puerto Rico, women in that region would be given a chance for the first time to work both outside the home and outside the cane fields. The little factories that soon dotted the Puerto Rican countryside probably did rather little, on balance, to rescue the rural sector.[24] But they gave women a chance to earn their own way, contributing substantially to the material improvement of many rural families. Over the years this also meant that women would be working, unchaperoned, and sometimes even in distant towns. My friend Paco (not his real name) had served in the U.S. army, was married by civil ceremony, worked as an accountant, probably used contraceptives, and was buying and building a house through Federal Housing Authority. His wife worked in a factory in a town a dozen miles away; she went there early each morning by local public taxi, returned each noon to make her spouse lunch—imagine that—and then went back to work until late afternoon.

I was talking to Paco one day, and I said "You know, twenty or thirty years ago, if I had told your father that the day would come in this barrio when wives would travel alone to work in distant towns for the entire day, he would have laughed in my face." Paco grew serious. "Look," he said, "we are building an expensive house. Our children are going to need more than eight years of schooling. We may need medical care someday. We need the two wages." "Oh, of course," I hastened to reply. "I was not criticizing. But you know, not far from Puerto Rico there is another island [I was thinking of Haiti], where country women make up large loads of farm produce and carry it by truck to the capital, and stay there two or three days retailing their wares, before returning home. Could you foresee something of that sort in Puerto Rico's future?" His face darkened in a mask of *macho* outrage. "If she is not in the house by four o'clock in the afternoon," he retorted, "I would lock the door."

Even though this exchange took place thirty-five years ago, it lets me make what may seem to be an obvious point: in matters of culture, persistences are at least as important as changes. Culturally, continuities and changes work in concert, so to speak; some ground is given here, retained there. Attitudes and values often survive in what seems to be an anachronistic manner. No culture ever remains exactly the same as it was before. Whether it be gender relations, race attitudes, or the dignity of the self, societies have a way of working out over time their distinctive solutions to such issues. Though those solutions are usually differentiated to at least some extent by such important intrasocietal differences as class and religion, as solutions they have long lives, are hardly ever made explicit and formulated as a code, and seem to underlie, unnoticed, large segments of behavior that we anthropologists have difficulty explaining. It may not be improper to add that some disciplines do not perceive these as questions worth asking. My own feeling is that the asking of such questions and the formulation of their answers is part of what the social sciences ought to do.

I use the term "solution" here to describe the way a social group or a society manages or copes with some contradiction, a difficulty, a question or "social problem," that requires at least a symbolic answer. These solutions often solve nothing concretely, on the ground; but they serve people, all the same, in enabling them to keep functioning; they enable things to go on "running." In discussing earlier how differently Jamaica and French Saint Domingue dealt with the emergence of large numbers of people of clearly heterogeneous origins, I was suggesting that they were "solving" differently a problem both of them faced. In what I am writing here, in connection with gender, say, or violence, or in what follows, on race relations, I seek to do more of the same: to provide some descriptive substance that can help us see better how such "solutions" are specific and particular.

Readers will recall the stress I have put on the differential demography of those Caribbean societies where the sugar industry developed intermittently and—in its "modern" form—late. Puerto Rico illustrates, perhaps best of all, that alternative pattern of population growth, in which the genetics of large numbers of inhabitants, in all likelihood a majority, includes physical signs of several populations of apparently differing origin. It is most of all in the Hispanic

Caribbean where one sees people whose appearance is reminiscent of the aboriginal inhabitants. That impression has a solid basis in contact history. The Puerto Rican people display a wide range of physical appearances, and the phenotypic features are classified by a large glossary of descriptive terms. Such lexicons are found everywhere in the Caribbean. But they are distinctive and specific and do not always describe the same things. For example, some Caribbean societies are much more concerned with hair form than others; and some are more dedicated to "lightening" their heritage. Class differences within any one such society seem also much to affect sensitivities to such differences. Puerto Ricans, like everyone else, have a lively awareness of these differences, and lengthy contact with North American society has, if anything, deepened that awareness. The so-called "one-drop rule" in the United States—the idea that if you're not white, you're black—fell on the Puerto Rican people with cruel force.[25] The Department of Defense invented the racial categories "Puerto Rican white" and "Puerto Rican colored" to handle their own North American problem with nonwhite people whom they were drafting or who enlisted in the army. As a result there were times when members of the same Puerto Rican family were assigned to different units of the army, which was segregated by "race." Nothing else, I think, that the United States ever did contributed so much to the movements for Puerto Rican independence in the years following World War II, and then the Korean War, than that impersonal, official, idiotic, and violent triumph of North American racism.

For the Puerto Rican people, as for many other (but definitely not all) societies south of the United States, there are not two (or three or four or whatever) races. Instead, there are *individuals,* who differ in their physical appearance. There are also categories (anthropologists' "folk categories," as if we recognized simultaneously the advantage of being indigenous and the disadvantage of not being "scientific"); and many individuals, if not all, can be described by *approximate* reference to those categories. Historically, the dominant (though surely not the only) racial polarity in the United States has been black-white. In Hispano-Caribbean societies, as in the United States, there exists the conception of there once having been two different populations that met and, to varying degrees, mixed. But there is also the idea—probably now changing, just as the governing North American perception of a black-white polarity is changing—of a gradient along which individuals may be "racially" identified and, often uncomfortably, self-identified as well. Against this gradient are projected a series of locally specific descriptive terms. These terms turn out to be short cuts to communication, but they serve to make less specific, rather than more, the gradient itself. Thus, for example, in Puerto Rico the term *trigueño* (wheat colored) is a euphemism for colored, and covers a wide range of complexions; the term *moreno* a euphemism for "colored [and negroid?] but not black";[26] while the term *negro* is not used to refer to race at all, at least in public. Anyone from North America or Europe who spends time in Puerto Rico in social situations dealing with people of widely varied appearance is likely to be struck by several different things at once. The social "tone" of so-called interracial relationships is likely to be warm and unburdened; the tension that so often creeps into such relationships in the United States is markedly absent. I supposed that the feeling white or light-skinned people have toward those who *look* black—that one should never be hurtful toward those darker than oneself—was a clue of a kind to local codes of racial etiquette. People appear to think that one can come in various shades, including "dark." But "dark" people are different from everyone else in a *different way* from the way light-skinned people are different from everyone else. In Puerto Rico "dark" people are the personae of the cartoons (e.g. *Diplo*) once popular in local journalism; and prominent dark people always seem to be treated, when seen, with favorable but exaggerated commentary. This, too, it seems to me, is an outcome of Puerto Rico's long and anciently intermixed history.

At the same time anecdotes, songs, and poems lay bare the fierce pride of family—of blood—that is called upon to surmount phenotypic distinctions. The feeling suffuses the lyrics of Vizcarrondo's *Y tu abuela—a'onde está?* There, one woman answers another who has publicly called her *negra.* "And your grandmother," she sings, "where is she?" The song makes a point about racial pride. The apocryphal story of the maid who is asked whether a certain Don Pedro is *negro* (a negro) makes a different point: some societies believe the gradient between black and white is almost infinitely long.[27]

The culturally specific recognition of a racial continuum from nonwhite to white in Puerto Rico has the odd concomitant effect, it seems to me, of sustaining racism there, and of frustrating political efforts to end it. To develop this theme fully (doubtless like others in my line of argument here) would be to write another book, I think. But in its briefest form, I would contend that the proliferation of color subcategories in Puerto Rico's racial system has made it impossible to create any group solidarity based on nonwhiteness; yet at the same time this way of classifying fails to protect those people who are darkest.

Puerto Rican migrants have often been startled, and some deeply distressed, to discover that North Americans perceive them as being in a category labeled "black."[28] As a very light-skinned blonde Puerto

Rican friend, one of the best students of race I know, said to me after her first visit to the mainland, "I didn't even know I was black till I came up here!" "Up here," we would say that she is white, or almost white, or some such thing. But we are also used to people who are white yet define themselves as black.[29] Even though we are accustomed to put all nonwhite people of whatever appearance in the same category, only changing the category name occasionally, it turns out that political mobilization around physical difference and sameness, around ethnic and "racial" categories, is an old, familiar, and often successful tactic in the United States.

It does not work in Puerto Rico. Racism lives on persistently there, and serious attempts to *expose* racist practices are regularly belittled as racist. It was once the case that any remonstrance in Puerto Rico over, say, difficulties in getting served in a restaurant would be met with considerable indignation. A headwaiter or manager or waiter might say to the victim's complaint: "Of what are you accusing me? Are you a racist?" In Puerto Rico, that is, explicit color-consciousness of the North American sort was punished. *Narciso descubre su trasero* (Narcissus discovers his behind), the book with this wonderful title by the late Isabelo Zenón Cruz, was enormously provocative in Puerto Rico when it was published because it shed light on the semisubterranean nature of Puerto Rican racism. It was a book the truth of which was, I think it can be said, carefully ignored by most of Puerto Rico's intelligentsia.

In Jauca, where there were many people of African—and sometimes Amerindian—appearance, social relations among workers seemed to me never visibly tense, and everyday conduct was unself-conscious and easy. My friend Taso, who was phenotypically white, had numerous compadres and comadres who were of mixed ancestry; his wife Elí's family was of mixed ancestry. My friends Gueni, Marcial, and Berto, all of whom would be defined as "black" in the U.S. (and two of whom would have been considered in that category in Puerto Rico), were Taso's compadres and comrades, intimate friends, deeply trusted, "like family." Physical contacts of all kinds between people of differing appearance were frequent and unremarkable. Marriages between two persons who differ greatly in their physical appearance along a white-black gradient are rare but do occur.[30] But those between two people who would be called white and black in the United States are unremarkable and very common.

In Puerto Rico, people who are dark in coloring or who have what Puerto Rican call "bad hair" *(pelo malo)* are aware, I think, of the dangers implicit in focusing attention on their own darkness. It was repeatedly and subtly indicated to me that if you did not do anything to acknowledge how dark you were, no one else would acknowledge it either. So the invisibility which Ralph Ellison associated with race in the United States is a different invisibility in Hispanic America. It is just as punitive (though of different behaviors) and works in a different manner.

In this connection, my friend Marcial's outlook toward his own identity bears note. The element of sadness it contained betrays, I believe, a racism that has remained, albeit much changed, in Puerto Rico. Its persistence is evidenced by the unwillingness of many of its victims to challenge it. A friend was recounting in Marcial's presence that as a young man Marcial had saved a girl's life at some risk to himself by bringing to a halt a runaway horse-drawn carriage. I tried to make a joke of it and said: "And so why were you not given the young lady's hand, after you saved her life?" Marcial took my remark quite seriously. "Ah, no," he said—"siendo yo triste de color, no sería posible." ("No, since I am sad of color, it would not be possible.") Where one might expect bitterness, there was sadness instead. The sometime nasty racism—looking like a historically understandable class hostility combined with the complex histories of complexion—that I detected in Jamaica seemed absent in Puerto Rico, where nearly everyone appeared instead to collude in denying the existence of racism altogether. But this is merely the deceptive outcome of a value system that has managed Puerto Rican race relations for centuries. The consequences must be measured particularly in how people are systematically deprived of economic opportunities, as well as in the psychological effects on people. The fact is that the cruelties of racism differ, within and between different cultures.

In a careful historical study of how visible physical differences have been used against Puerto Ricans over time, Kinsbruner (1996) analyzed the available materials on residential patterns, family organization, and known history to analyze the fates of nonwhite inhabitants of San Juan, particularly for the period 1823–46. Though the data are limited and require much inference, the picture he paints is one in which free people of color enjoyed some pretty solid legal protection but there was serious economic discrimination against them. Kinsbruner calls attention to three particularly egregious documents that also discriminated against people of color. They symbolized the eighteenth and nineteenth centuries, which I view as that long concluding period during which poor rural Puerto Ricans of all sorts learned to work alongside each other even while the fates of nonwhite Puerto Ricans were being turned against them. The warmth of social relations, the apparent lack of tension, the broad acceptance of difference, all of which have made Puerto Rican race relations less toxic, have nonetheless done nothing for the economic and political equality of all people of color.

I have set forth here some of what I perceive as provocative sociological differences among my cases. Some of the differences flow from different economic and hence demographic differences. Others, it seems to me, may have transatlantic origins. I should conclude this chapter on the third ancient colony by stressing again that what I offer here are my impressions only; and to do so, I have looked back half a century. I am, in short, describing a world that has gone on changing, for example a Puerto Rico now denuded of sugarcane and much that went with it. I will turn back to Puerto Rico yet again, though briefly, in the concluding chapter.

5

Creolization, Culture, and Social Institutions

IN THIS BOOK I have tried to build a picture of the Caribbean region in which the description of local variation rests on a broad historical view. Then I sought to fill in that picture by discussing three ancient colonies in which the nature of the local variant might be explored. The reader will have noted that what I describe in the latter part of each of the last three chapters is based mainly on things I learned from my own fieldwork.

I meant these chapters to offer something that goes a little beyond the simply descriptive. I think of the world as having been remade, gradually, intermittently, and over the course of centuries, into an enormous but incomplete network of connections of all kinds. There have been periods of intense contraction, with a shrinkage of contacts and a relocalization of activity. But these have been followed by new movements, set off by big technological advances, by demographic shifts, and often by periods of peace and coalition building. By looking at that ongoing multiplex history, we can see how whole regions might be transformed from quiet backwaters into key centers of intense economic activity, usually in response to ever more intrusive external forces. Political power, technology, sometimes the showing and use of violence have been used to alter profoundly the currents and flow patterns that mark the growth of new centers of production or new markets, remaking the economic significance of particular geographic locales.[1]

I think that the emergence of the Caribbean region centuries ago as a critical center of such flow patterns is only one of many such examples. Regions, it is often pointed out these days, are not eternal verities but are defined and redefined as geographical precipitates of particular forces (Hollander 2008). What regions are often defined by turns in part on what the world takes from them and brings to them. Much of this book is concerned with just such things. I began by noting that in the sixteenth century, the barely touched natural resources of the Caribbean region—its physiography, soil, timber, water, climate, location—made it ideal for the introduction of plantations and such plants as the sugarcane. Without those added resources, it could not have become what it became. Such a region can lose or gain economic preeminence in response to the presence and play of external forces, in relation to its existing endowments. That was true of this region as well.

When some previously unknown or only weakly defended territory has been seized, then a new potential kind of wealth in agriculture or in animal breeding, a previously unused local resource, or some powerful technological innovation can be given room to take shape, within wider systems of exchange. To study how such changes have actually occurred in specific New World examples is one way of calling attention to the many and varied pasts still traceable within the "new" hemisphere (see e.g., Bauer 2001; Friedmann 1999; Friedmann and McMichael 1989; Mintz and Friedmann 2004; Wolf 1982). In this book I wanted to uncover aspects of those Caribbean pasts.

For centuries, the region of which I write was a magnet for European power and ambition. For more than two hundred years, Eric Williams tells us (1944), every important European naval engagement was fought in and for the Caribbean. The Caribbean, that is, really mattered. Following the Seven Years' War, and in order to reclaim its former colonies Guadeloupe and Martinique, France reluctantly decided to forgo its claims to Canada. Think of that—its claims to Canada. Anyone who looks at a map or has visited a Caribbean island will be stunned by the very idea of such an exchange. Canada, joked Voltaire, has nothing but fur—fur and acres and acres of snow. But the Antilles, he added—the Antilles have sugar. On those little islands it was as if they had planted gold. But the crop was fertilized with the blood of human beings.

I have dwelt at such length on the role of labor in the history of the Antilles mostly (though not only) because I have had slave labor especially in mind. It is nearly incredible that these small islands could have swallowed up so many people. Eltis (2000:11) calculates that for the years 1580–1760—that is, from near the beginning of the Atlantic trade until the period of the second, mostly nineteenth-century plantation explosion in the Caribbean—captive Africans made up between two-thirds and three-fourths of the total number of migrants to the New World.

Their forced labor led to the accumulation of enormous wealth. I noted earlier that Saint Domingue may have been, at least for a few decades, quite possibly modernity's most lucrative colony. Outstanding examples of European architecture, such as the Codrington Library at All Souls' College, Oxford, and Jamaica plantation owner William Beckford's palatial Fonthill Splendens, in Wiltshire, were built out of stolen labor power, in these cases mainly in the British Caribbean. Yet once the wealth itself was made and reinvested elsewhere; once those precious tropical commodities could be produced even more cheaply on islands in a different ocean; once the nature of the link between metropolis and colony began to change—the raging Caribbean economic fire burned down to embers, and most of the islands became bedraggled reminders of colonial splendor.

Much later, some islands, such as Puerto Rico and Cuba and later the Dominican Republic, would be made part of a different economic bloc, this time under U.S. tutelage. But the region as a whole had by then lost its former luster. Most of the islands, once greatly coveted, were now little more than annoyances to their imperial masters. Though the region may never lose its place in U.S. geopolitical thinking—migration, drugs, Fidel Castro, Duvalier, offshore banking, Grenada, Guantánamo—it will never again weigh so heavily in European colonial imaginings. These islands are a place of past glories, of long-dead pirates and crumbling ruins, of music and poverty, much as the tourist descriptions proclaim them to be.

But that is certainly not all that they are. They have *people,* too, with social systems and cultures, aesthetic preferences, enormous talent, brilliant scholarship, and utterly remarkable opinions and insights on the world. Two Nobel laureates (one in literature, one in economics) have come from the tiny island of St. Lucia; the list of gifted Caribbean individuals is quite out of proportion to the population of their region. But my aim here was not to represent these islands, only to try to fit the everyday people whom I knew into what I understood of their history, a history no longer present, if not yet quite past.

In all three of the ancient places I studied, slavery, race, and race relations were important both in local history and in people's consciousness, but not to the same degree or with the same intensity in all of them. These bulky (and sometimes disagreeable) topics have surfaced often in the preceding text because slavery was such a core feature of the regional economy. The slaves when they came were different culturally and physically from their captors, and the differing demographic and sociological consequences of slavery in each case helped to endow these societies with much of their distinctive identities. I have tried to make clear that slavery mattered as the accompaniment to a particular form of agricultural organization. But though it lay at the heart of the social system in some of these places, in others it was minor, or arrived later, or did not take on quite the same form. In the three societies with which I have been concerned here, it should be clear that slavery was least important in the history of Puerto Rico. I shall try to suggest later in this chapter that the Hispanic Caribbean societies, Puerto Rico included, stand apart historically in some ways from the rest of their neighbors.

The geographic poles of New World slavery were Brazil and the United States. In those two huge societies, the plantation past, slavery, and race deeply affected governance and economic and social relations. But in these big countries, the effects were experienced more in particular regions than nationally. Obviously I am not trying to say that slavery was not critically important to the history of either Brazil or the United States. But the tangle of forces I have been describing here, though very important, was not central to all of the major events in the histories of those enormous states. In contrast, the Caribbean islands were small places—small enough so that they could be launched headlong, by imperial decisions made elsewhere, on some particular course. Remote but powerful forces could deeply affect their entire destinies because they were so small and because they remained colonial for so long.

In two cases, Jamaica and Saint Domingue (Haiti), I noted that there was not enough infrastructure in place once slavery ended and that there had been too little preparation for building a new kind of society based on citizenship instead of the whip. In Saint Domingue, years of invasion, war, revolution, and afterward foreign vindictiveness made reconstruction especially difficult. In contrast to these cases, Puerto Rico, affected later in time and much less profoundly by the plantation complex, evolved quite differently.

I want to enlarge on those differences here by looking at a theoretical concept I think is linked closely to Caribbean identity. It can be used to explain much of what happened culturally to those societies in which a large majority of people was enslaved and confined to the sugar plantations over very lengthy periods. This concept may also provide a way of comparing the three ancient colonies. The concept is creolization. It has been given new importance and new meanings in recent years. I want to try to rethink it here.

I have now said many times that the three colonial societies I describe here were subjected to similar large historical forces but not to the same extent. They were pioneer societies, and the plantations were pioneer institutions within them.[2] Peopled from afar and consigned to modern economic uses, these places came to represent a kind of world frontier in their time. The newcomers to these societies were culturally heterogeneous. In two of them, Jamaica and Saint Domingue, and over the course of a century or more, nearly all of the newcomers were enslaved. Violence and its constant threat served to keep such people under control. Because of these conditions, imposed as they were on culturally and linguistically heterogeneous groups of captives, each society served as an incubator of social innovation. Once again, I believe that this was least true of

Puerto Rico. But in order to say more of what I think happened culturally in these plantation frontiers, though, I should first indicate what I think the terms "creole" and "creolization" mean.

Both are commonly used with reference to the Caribbean region. But I do not believe they refer to the same thing. The oldest meaning of "creole" has to do with the way the New World filled up over time with people and things of Old World origin. "Creole" meant something of the Old World born in the New. Though many other meanings have been added and others lost in the course of centuries, that central idea persisted. In English—and there are equivalents in other languages—the child of African slaves born in the New World was a "creole." His or her parents were "salt-water" or "Guinea" Negroes. The term *bozal,* in Spanish, *bossal* in French, had the same meaning of coming from elsewhere (also of being wild and untamed). But pigs, chickens, and other things whose ancestors came from elsewhere were also "creole" if they were born in the Americas, not imported. The term eventually came to refer also to New World societies of mixed cultures or "races"—perhaps particularly those where one human ingredient was African in origin. But as an adjective, it appears that "creole" was more commonly attached to some societies of the Americas than to others: to Latin America rather than America north of Mexico (New Spain); to the Caribbean islands; to Louisiana; and to foods, drinks, dances, people, religions, and so on connected to those places.

It is worth noting that while the original meaning referred to the results of the movement of people and things to the Americas, the commoner meaning today usually carries the idea of mixing or blending. Strikingly, in that usage there seems to be no clear-cut distinction between what is cultural and what biological. This secondary meaning overlaps to some extent with such terms as the Spanish *mestizo* or *cholo,* or the French term *métis,* used to refer to people of mixed origins. And when people refer in English to "creoles" or to a "creole" region or country, often they mean or imply people who are not wholly Caucasian or the places where such people live. This broadening usage makes less sense to me. If "creole" *only* means something of the Old World born in the New, then any country in the New World is, or was, a creole country at one time; and everyone born in any such country (except Native Americans) is or was a creole.

There is, however, one use of "creole" as a noun or adjective that seems to me to escape from that problem. This usage is faithful to the original meaning of the word, and its meaning has not been wholly diluted. That is when the word refers to a language—a creole language. I will take up that meaning later. But first I want to offer a definition of creolization.

The term "creolization" is relatively new and has been given various meanings, nowadays mostly associated with cultural change. It probably was first used to describe the process by which a new language was created in the interaction between slaves and masters, a process thought of as similar to the creation of trade languages. In recent years the meaning of the word has been moved away from language in particular and greatly broadened so as to make it applicable to societies elsewhere outside the Americas (e.g., Hannerz 1987, 1992; Stewart 2007).

In spite of this broadening of meaning, I believe that what creolization means is best revealed when applied to a particular process of change that unfolded in the Caribbean region during the history of slavery and the sugar plantation. I think the conditions that led to creolization, then and there, were almost unique in the human social record. I will question the grounds on which the three ancient colonies I have described in this book can be called creolized (as opposed to "creole"). I will argue that the process of creolization applied to only two of them: French Saint Domingue (Haiti) and Jamaica.

I think of creolization, in contradistinction to creole, as the creative cultural synthesis undertaken primarily by the slaves, interacting with each other and with free people, including the master class, particularly in the tropical New World sugar plantation colonies. By this synthesis, new social institutions, furnished with reordered cultural content, were forged to provide a basis for continuing cultural growth.[3]

By specifying creolization's meaning this way I mean to reduce, not expand it. In doing so, I think I can make clear both some things these three ancient colonies shared and some they did not, especially with regard to the conditions that provided the context for creolization.

All three of these societies underwent plantation development at one time or another. In all three, sugar plantations were the most important estates producing commodities for European markets. In all three, sugar had been produced by slaves early in their history under the Spaniards. But the quantities were negligible at first, and relatively little was exported. Nearly all of the slaves in all three colonies were enslaved Africans, to whom were soon added their slave descendants (who would be described as "creoles").[4]

In each case, newly enslaved people were brought into the colony in varying numbers over the course of centuries, influencing the ongoing social and cultural relations among the inhabitants of each colony.[5] Yet as I have tried to show, plantation slavery played a quite different part in the social, economic, and political life of each society over time, ending under entirely different conditions in each: by revolution in Saint Domingue (1804); by act of the British Parliament in Jamaica (1834 or 1838); and by Spanish law in Puerto Rico, where it had become economically minor (1873 or 1876). The social relations obtaining between the slaves and the free people, both colored and white, differed as well in all three societies.

It is a platitude that all societies change over time. But *creolization*, as opposed to *being* creole, was a process that unfolded mostly during that half century or so when the first large introductions of enslaved Africans were occurring in these islands. "First half century" here refers to a historical stage, not to some particular fifty years. For most of Caribbean history as I see it, creolization was associated with northern European (British, Dutch, French, and possibly Danish) plantation activity, none of which began before the seventeenth century. Creolization was not an event, occurring in one place at one time; it occurred at different times, in different places. But I think it occurred in the same way in different places and times, with similar consequences. Hence what I think of as the creolization episodes were not synchronic but systadial: a similar stage taking place at different times and in different places (Mintz 1964; 1979:220 and n.12; 2002:355–356).

My view is that not every Caribbean colony went through a creolization process. I believe that there were founding conditions that surrounded and shaped creolization. I have mentioned slavery and plantations in particular. But there is more. Plantations were established in the New World mostly in places where the Europeans, intentionally or not, had killed off the native populations. In the

Caribbean in particular, plantations were founded in lands not so much empty as *emptied*. Moreover, with the start of colonial domination, both master and slave were foreign newcomers (Mintz 1966). This meant that such repeopling involved two different groups: one smaller, politically dominant, culturally and linguistically homogeneous; the other soon becoming far larger, subordinate, culturally heterogeneous, and usually with speakers of different languages among them.[6]

Using "creole" to mean a language is a very old practice. I've mentioned that the term "creolization," used to describe a creative or productive process of change, first arose in connection with language. Creole languages caught the attention of linguists long ago and became subjects of serious study during the last century (e.g., Reinecke 1964; Schultze 1933). Creolists have been debating many issues concerning these languages ever since. I think most of the issues—the possible role of African pidgins in the formation of New World creole languages; the role of Caribbean creole languages in any broader category of trade languages; universal linguistic processes versus other processes in creole language formation; and so on—are not questions for which definitive answers are needed for the present argument. Understanding the social contexts in which creole languages did or did not emerge, however, can help to clarify for us what creolization as a larger social process really meant (Mintz 1971a).[7]

Reinecke made quite clear, seventy years ago, why these strange tongues could prove to be so sharp a diagnostic of local sociology and history: "unless the slave population was overwhelmingly in the majority and fairly stable of residence (conditions obtaining especially on the sugar cane–growing islands), only the initial makeshift jargon was spoken; or if a creole dialect did form, it was soon ironed out.... Especially in the Hispanic colonies, where manumission was common and the freedmen were often merged socially and racially with the whites, conditions were unfavorable to the consolidation of a creole dialect" (1964:540). The late great Dutch sociologist Harmannus (Harry) Hoetink reasoned similarly. He contended that from the first—and in spite of the horrors the Spaniards had visited on Native American peoples in the early centuries—the social homogeneity of Hispanophone Caribbean societies stood out in sharp contrast to the social systems of the other colonial powers. What he wrote is of particular interest to me because he starts not with the societies but with their languages:

> The best illustration of this [social] homogenization is probably provided by the fact that in all Latin Caribbean societies the language of the Iberian mother country became the commonly spoken and written language, while in virtually none of the societies of the North-West European variant is one language the official as well as the common language. In Haiti, French is the official language, Creole the common one; in the British West Indies English is the official language and Anglo-Creole or French Creole the common one; in the French islands, French and French-Creole, respectively; in the Dutch Windward Islands, English or Dutch and Anglo-Creole; in Surinam, Dutch and Sranang (apart from the Asian languages); in the Dutch Leeward Islands, Dutch and Papiamentu. The linguistic situation in the North-West European variant reflects the cleavage which has always existed between the original dominant segment and the great majority of non-whites, while in the Iberian variant the lin-

guistic situation reflects the linking function of the colored group. (Hoetink 1967:178)

This is an eloquent argument that deals with the *social* significance of a linguistic fact. It presumes (I think correctly) that the absence of a creole language in the Hispanic colonies is good evidence that Spanish either was or became the language of everyone right from the start. So the absence of creole languages in the Hispanic Caribbean says something about the social communities in the Hispanic Caribbean into which slaves entered and within which their children grew up (hence something, too, about the demography of those places); and something, finally, about the social roles of people who were intermediate in both physique and social status in those colonies. The clear inference is that people of mixed physical origins spoke Spanish as did everyone else, and that African newcomers learned Spanish from them. Most important for the social scientist: here we see language has a lively relevance for penetrating the different social contexts within which slaves lived and settled.

From its establishment in the New World onward, the sugar plantation became a meeting ground for people speaking many different languages—on one side several or many different African languages, on the other side a European language such as French, English, Dutch, or Danish. The plantations required communication between slaves and masters so that work would be done. What became the medium of communication between these two groups was a language, perhaps restricted in some ways, that made possible what needed to be communicated.

These are often referred to as trade languages, specialized for trade and work. Their European names, including *Sklavensprachen* (slave languages; Schultze 1933:378–381) suggest their common association with particular conditions of social life and labor. Such languages arose out of the work situation and they could serve as a lingua franca when the slaves had no language in common. It has been supposed that they expanded lexically after the birth of children, who (unlike any newly arrived, enslaved Africans) lacked any native language. These emergent and presumably enriched languages were creoles. They came to be spoken generally, were taught to children, and thus became indigenous. "Creolization" was first employed as a label to describe the development of those creole tongues. The majority view now seems to be that at least some creole languages evolved swiftly, without any preceding pidgin or the need for a generation of creole infants for their expansion. Many, probably most, languages called creoles in the world today are Caribbean; in some cases (notably Haiti but not only there) creole is the language of everyone.

The social (or sociological) importance of these languages cannot be exaggerated, for they are our best example of the creolization process. These were languages created by the slaves, first in minimal interaction with nonslaves and thereafter among themselves.[8] Understanding the social conditions under which such languages arise is crucial to our understanding the creolization of language. Karttunen and Crosby (1995:165), for example, suggest that creole languages have arisen in situations of *catastrophe*, in which advances in transport technology made it possible to move large numbers of people to unpopulated places, where they had little contact with people other than themselves.

I also think there are grounds for using Caribbean creole languages as models, however sketchy, for inferring what *cultural* creolization was like. Our evidence for how cultural creolization took shape is far less systematic than that for languages. The founding conditions I think include empty (or emptied) lands and the means to get enslaved people to them; two groups that differed in size, language characteristics, and power; the creation of large overseas estates where the labor force was made up entirely of the larger group (and none of the smaller); and the enslaved status of that larger group.

I claim that the same conditions that apply to the emergence of creole languages applied with equal or greater force to the emergence of creolized cultures (Mintz 1971a). I claim this by analogy only. The difficulty in making such a case arises from the relatively systematic nature of language and the absence of such systematicity in culture—and perhaps the inadequacy of anthropological theory. But I think the case has to be made.

In Chapter 1, I claimed that Caribbean plantations had specific effects on the people who were dragged across oceans in chains to work on them. I suggested that the destruction of their familial, community, religious, and other links to time, place, and culture, when combined with the anonymity and alienation of their lives and the conditions of their labor, produced fundamental changes in their outlook and personality. Like some others, I think of the aggregate effects of these changes as a misbegotten kind of modernization. I want to enlarge on those assumptions here by trying to describe what happened.

The enslaved came from many different African societies but mainly from West Africa. In their majority they were from farming and animal-keeping (not pastoral, and not solely hunting) societies— that is, they were mostly people stolen from settled agricultural villages or else were war captives, many from within larger political entities. Highly productive indigenous farming systems had led to big populations in much of West Africa. Among the enslaved and transported there were speakers of scores of different languages. Men, women, and children, they came from all of the different social levels of the societies to which they had belonged. Some had been prisoners of war, others debt slaves; occasionally there was a member of an indigenous ruling family—a prince or princess. Probably most of the captives were villagers—perhaps distantly like today's Africans—who were assaulted by thieves of humans while farming, collecting firewood, and fetching water for the evening meal: people who were living peaceful and productive lives.

Once the Atlantic trade was firmly established, most victims were seized and bargained over by professional slave catchers and carried off in "coffles" (from the Arabic, meaning "caravan"), stumbling down to the coast in long, manacled lines to be resold abroad. They were shipped to the Americas under famously horrifying conditions. A great number—estimated at 10 to 15 percent—died or were killed on the way. The survivors ended up in the slave markets of the Americas.

I want to call attention to three principal ideas or themes in what follows. First, creolization was a reaction of people to the terrible constraints of enslavement and the concomitant ethnic disorganization—an attempt by the victims to respond creatively to their condition. As such, it was part of the universal human need to make daily life meaningful. Second, I contend that to do so, they had to build collective social institutions within slavery. Simply to remember their own past, while crucial, was not enough. Memories had to be aggregated collectively to build shared social practices. Such processes of rebuilding, of informing daily lives with new meanings, were modernizing experiences. Finally, so profound was the cultural disruption caused by enslavement and social randomization that the creolization process that followed became a rich but unrecognized source of understanding for any theory of human culture.

It should be noted once again that slaves did sometimes come from culturally similar groups, sometimes even from the same group; and there is good evidence here and there of transatlantic continuity. I am not contending this never happened, only that it was neither common nor predominant.

My aim here is to discuss the initial situation—whenever it occurred in historical time—in which two foreign populations, one monolingual and powerful, the other nearly powerless and multilingual, interacted on a daily basis. The enslaved had been dragged together from different places and from culturally different groups, with members of both sexes and all ages. Save for newborn infants, each person had a name, was a family member, spoke a language (or more than one), lived in a community he or she called home, and occupied social statuses, as farmer or soldier or housekeeper or smith, domestic slave or prince. They were brothers and sisters, sons and daughters, father and mothers, to others. Each such individual had been socialized into the statuses one acquires through birth or achievement (one's kinfolk by birth, one's language and trade mostly by achievement). Most would carry, in hand and heart and head, memories of before, skills and songs, and lots of ideas about the proper way to do this and that: to eat, to greet, to court, to pray, to care for children, to make love—even to gesture, to walk, to smile.

Every passing moment in life involves such knowledge, including the knowledge by which new members of the society are led into a culturally specific identity. There are things that have to be done with a newborn boy child to legitimate it, protect it, and fix its status in its family, village, and society. It is the same (or different) with a girl child, and it may be different for twins. There is a right number of wives, but it may vary with rank. The names for the newborn may be prescribed by custom. Special birthmarks may bring special status; and so on, and on. Thousands of such known things and practices, and possibly hundreds of thousands—learned, remembered, filed away in each person's mind. This enormous accumulation of ways for being and living, which nested within the mentalities of the enslaved, was merely irrelevant nonsense from the perspective of the masters. But it had been the very substance of everyday life for the slaves.

The creolization process was effectuated socially, and it involved millions of ordinary people of these kinds, everywhere that plantation slavery developed swiftly and with momentum. Those "ordinary" people—young and old, strong and weak, clever and slow, angry and submissive—were obliged, probably only more or less consciously and deliberately, to figure out how to retain and restructure their humanity under the most trying conditions in world history. What they achieved took most of all work—social interaction, resourcefulness, inventiveness. It was a collective, *social* kind of uniquely human achievement. Each bit of that achievement was put in place by individuals; but the causes and consequences of creolization were inherently social in their significance, and group decisions surely played an important part in the outcomes.

Slaves often died within a year, from maltreatment, illness, and overwork. They were forced to work. No one provided any opportunity in which they could try to recreate life as they remembered it. Yet they were in a situation where they had to solve *their* problems instantly. Amid their disorientation and suffering, babies were born and people died. What is more, people flirted and fell in love. Later in world history, people would do the same in the concentration camps. The immediacy of necessity and of feeling was an ever-present twin aspect of the oppression of the slaves, as it would one day be of the concentration and death camps. Slavery on the plantations and life in the concentration camps both provide evidence as well, of what looks like a seemingly universal human necessity for some assurance that people are doing the right things, socially.

In the forging of African-American traditions, as in the whole of human history, we learn that all people, anywhere and all of the time, are motivated to do things that endow daily life with meaning. Berger writes of us humans that we are "congenitally compelled to impose a meaningful order upon reality" (1967:22). I think this means human beings must have ways to deal with events that lack intrinsic meaning for them. Until they are able to *create* order (and hence meaning) to explain what they are doing, and why, their lives remain meaningless.

The enslaved lost enormous quantities of those parts of their ancestral cultures that were connected to how things are done. Knowing how to behave in particular cultural terms was being taken from them. Knowing why we behave in those ways—often revealed to us only as we continue to do them—was also melting away. People need the assurance that they—as well as others like them—are doing the right things, socially. But when many different cultures are represented in the same setting, then *which set* of right things? It must be repeatedly brought to mind that in most of the situations we are considering, people from many different culturally specific societies had been thrown together randomly and now had to build new institutions collectively.

The second point about creolization, then, is about building social institutions within which cultural material from many sources, if necessary, could be installed. That means mixing materials, yes, into new syntheses. But it is not primarily about mixing—like using heavy cream rather than light cream with coffee. It is about achieving a new synthesis for people who are culturally diverse. First, the losses; then, building to replace them by mixing and synthesizing. I think it is misleading to put the primary emphasis on mixing. Such mixing is a common phenomenon whenever two cultures interpenetrate or share a border. Anthropologists used to call it "culture change," or "acculturation," until the term "culture" itself was rather haughtily discarded. To speak first of creolization as hybridization, mixing, exchanging, or trading is to diminish the genuinely reconstructive, creative, synthesizing aspect of these processes. It seems to me to detach the social objectives of the synthesis—what people were trying to achieve—from the synthesis itself.

In trying to define creolization, I used the word "institution." I spoke of creolization as cultural synthesis by means of which new institutions with "reordered" cultural content were established. I use the word "institution" here in an ordinary, textbook sense: an organization such as a church, a practice such as courtship.[9] By "culture," I mean here a resource—a pool of learned ideas, beliefs, customs, understandings—on which people draw in dealing with daily life. But for people in a culture to live and to enact their culture, they

202 · THREE ANCIENT COLONIES

need institutions. Drawing this distinction is important to our understanding of what was happening to the enslaved once they were on the plantations. Cultural perpetuation requires not simply the cultural materials but also institutions—social platforms, latticeworks of and for interaction—that help to sustain cultural materials over time and to give more exact shape to them through social practice. Most of those materials need the ongoing social behavior of people—actors—to maintain and perpetuate them.

That is not true of all cultural materials. Many words, proverbs, songs, and so on were carried from Africa to the New World by individual persons who could transmit them to others even without a common language (Warner-Lewis 2003). But to a large extent those poignant cultural substances could become part of a community's practices only through the constitution of groups that could use them in socially collective behavior, thus retaining, standardizing, or changing them. Of course institutions change over time, and in response to economic, political, or other pressures. But some distinction between institution and culture (expressed in many different forms) seems to me essential to any intelligent discussion of creolization.

The joining together of culture and institutions is often absent from discussions of the African-American heritage. When institutions are part of the picture, they are normally the centerpiece (e.g., a religious cult group, a revolving credit association). The institutional history—how cultural content is fitted within a structure of action—is taken for granted and not even referred to as such. But the cultural detail within such an institution is much less problematic than the creation of the institution itself.[10]

The captive Africans arriving in the New World were able to bring parts of their ancestral cultures with them. Most of all, it was what they remembered, including language, motor habits, and other culturally inscribed material. Memory was central. But often there was no one, or very few persons, with whom the individual captive could communicate freely. Their capacity to transfer cultural materials that depended on some sort of social organization—not a religion but its priesthood; not iron working but a guild of smiths; not a regal tradition but a royal lineage—was cruelly narrowed by enslavement and transportation.

By contrast, in the Massachusetts Bay colony, for instance, the white newcomers from the British Isles had a greater opportunity to perpetuate cultural materials because they came in groups, spoke one language and usually worshiped the same god. They brought musical instruments, some of their foods, and even their tastes in clothing and furniture. They kept their holidays. Yet even in these far more favorable conditions, they were quite unable to preserve every object and tradition. The wrenching changes in their daily life had direct cultural consequences. Learning to eat maize, squash, beans, turkey, and codfish, to live among local native people who were culturally and linguistically as different as can be, under weather conditions and on terrain very different from home, meant changing. What they could do was reestablish their churches, found their towns on the same political practices, install their educational system: that is, *ground their institutions*.

When people are moved great distances, even under the best circumstances, they find it hard to maintain their institutions unchanged. When those being moved are not themselves all from the same society or have the same culture, the difficulties increase for all of them; all are more vulnerable to the power of alien institutions.

So did those millions of oppressed people "lose" their cultures or become cultureless, as the ideology of slavery claimed? Of course not. Enslavement, transportation, and the plantation regimen were profoundly disturbing to the original institutions of the enslaved, who came from many societies. But these catastrophes did not succeed in wiping clean the memory and creativity of the enslaved. Memory, creativity, and collective effort made possible the reinstitutionalization of African-American lifeways.

The choices people made would be of those practices that might win consensus within a group, insofar as groups were taking shape— practices that might become normative, making it possible for an institution (for courtship, or marriage, or ritual postnatal protection for the newborn, or funerary practice) *to work*. I believe the dispersion of enslaved Africans from their original local groups left limited opportunities for an exact reconstitution of a remembered past.

I have already suggested that creolization modernized Caribbean people. This is not an original idea, but it is a commonly ignored one. Caribbean peoples were modernized by enslavement, by forced transportation in large, ethnically mixed groups, by massing in time-conscious enterprises, by the reshuffling of gender roles, by constant oppression, and by the need to reconstitute their cultural forms anew, and under pressure. This was happening to people from societies of a different sort from the ones into which they were brought; they were thrust into what were remarkably industrial settings for their time, with their smokestacks, mills and raging fires. Finally, they were controlled primarily by physical violence. They learned how to live under constant repression. It is for these reasons and these forces, acting continuously and in concert, that Caribbean cultures took on what I call a remarkably modern cast for their time.

Many culturally different peoples, at a different point in their histories, were thrust into a world they could not wholly reject and stay alive; a world they had to deal with in which they had become interchangeable units of labor, stripped of all kinship but the nuclear family (and at first, of that as well); and subjected to conditions of social life that, beyond the whip, they had to create for themselves.

My claim that the phenomenon of creolization contributes to our study of cultural theory rests on the concept of culture, as anthropologists have used the term: culture, first, as a universal, uniquely human possession; second, culture as understandable in terms of the social organization of behavior within distinguishable human groups.[11] In the whole of world history I know of no destruction, both of cultures and of institutions, whose consequences can vie in scale or intensity with those of Atlantic slavery. The American anthropologist Alfred Kroeber wrote that how culture comes to be is really more distinctive of culture than what it is (Kroeber 1948:253). Creolization, as the process by which slaves dealt with the immediate postenslavement trauma they faced, comes as close to understanding how culture comes to be than anything else in the human record I know of.

But this is not a book of anthropological theory. My purpose is simply to attempt on paper to restore to creolization what I think must have been its original meaning. Fortunately, definitions cannot be legislated; nor should they be. But I think that the enlargement of the word "creolization" into an umbrella term for widely variant types of culture change has snatched from the African-American experience its extraordinary significance in world history. Used in this way, it has also had the effect of ironing out the many varied contemporary experiences now being described as "creolized" (Mintz 1996, 1997). Since "creolization" refers to a particular historical process, it is worth enumerating the major characteristics of what it once meant in particular and specific detail.

While I was in Puerto Rico in 1948–1949, my reading made me aware of that island's "deviant" history compared to that of the category of so-called sugar islands. I was doing my fieldwork there during the heyday of the modern sugar plantations, and much the same was true then of Cuba and the Dominican Republic. All three Hispanic places were caught up at that time in the world sugar economy, under North American tutelage. But I knew that all three had shared much of their early history. When places like Jamaica and French Saint Domingue were becoming classic "sugar islands," the colonial darlings of their metropolises, the Hispanic islands had remained "backward" or "underdeveloped," relatively remote from the world economy of the sixteenth and seventeenth centuries.

I have already described what happened to Jamaica and Saint Domingue. Wherever the drive to create a flourishing, slave-based sugar plantation economy succeeded—with big ongoing importations of enslaved Africans, enormous enterprises with scores or even hundreds of slaves, and regimens of labor maintaining iron discipline with daily cruelties of all sorts—the process of creolization was set in motion. This was the way African Americans were created out of the "salt-water niggers." I had not realized that that was what creolization really meant.

In the Hispanic islands in the seventeenth century, things were not quite like that. Yes, the plantations, the slaves, and the sugarcane had all been tried there under Spain's rule (as well as in Jamaica and Santo Domingo and Cuba). The plantations had been established in the early years of the sixteenth century, manned by enslaved Africans, no doubt as maltreated as any. But those plantations failed; and repeated attempts to restore them led to no huge plantation growth or steady slave importations comparable to what Spain's rivals would achieve after 1650. Puerto Rico fitted perfectly into the Hispanic triad. This is not to say that Puerto Rico's slave owners were any more humane than those elsewhere in the Antilles. Economic failure did not lead to some miraculous appearance of improved human feeling. But economic failure led to manumission as a way of economizing, and manumission to a new demography, and a new demography to the chance to create a different human landscape, a different sort of social identity.

Between the stagnation of Puerto Rico's sugar industry after 1650 and its virtual rebirth in the early decades of the nineteenth century,[12] Puerto Rican rural life took on a very different appearance from that of the northern European sugar islands. I have indicated in broad outline for Puerto Rico a picture of a rural landscape with few towns; many subsistence cultivators; ranchers and resident laborers; people raising cattle, growing ginger, and selling hides and spices by boat; everyone—or nearly everyone—a free person; probably a majority of people of mixed physical appearance; runaways, including runaway slaves from other islands seeking refuge in the interior, and not being chased; and apparently no one much under the thumb of the colonial government or the city, except the city dwellers.

There are some inferences in what I have written here. But I have no doubt that Puerto Rico was more like Santo Domingo and Cuba than it was like the colonies of northern Europe. In that same connection, I deem it important that those rural people—and at least in broad terms, their only urban neighbors, in San Juan—shared a common culture, based largely on what had been brought to the New World—and then partly lost—by the Spanish conquerors from the 1500s onward. The absence of the very economic and political forces that had turned so many Caribbean colonies into vast estates filled with enslaved Africans, a few all-powerful Europeans, continuing floods of new slaves, and almost maddened activity in the fields and mills left places like Puerto Rico looking—and indeed being— very different.

Yet I think that the distinctiveness of the Hispanic Caribbean may go even further. Indeed, among the important regional distinctions to be drawn today among Caribbean societies, from the perspective of anthropology or political science, a major one is that between the Hispanic Antilles and the rest. My argument in this regard is based on quite simple differences.

All three Hispanic societies failed to develop the explosive adaptations based on slavery, plantations, and sugar that typified Spain's northern European colonial rivals in the region during the period 1650–1800. As a consequence, none of the three took on the characteristic nearly all-slave, all-African character of the "sugar islands." Because they did not, none experienced creolization as I have described it. (What happened in Cuba after 1792, when sugar became king there, raises different questions but not, I think, this question.)

An additional consequence was the absence of any deep fissure between the poor and the white—a fissure in the creolized sugar islands that was reflected in language, culture, and nearly everything else. The Hispanic islands remained underdeveloped and culturally and linguistically much more unitary. In part they are more homogeneous because they share a common Hispanic heritage. But they share a common Hispanic heritage because the whites who came to them mostly came to stay; and the nonwhites who were brought there came in small enough numbers, and over a long enough time, that they could be successfully integrated into that heritage. This happened in spite of their origins, and to a startling extent in spite of their economically more underprivileged status. Hispano-Caribbean societies are more alike not only because they share so many cultural features but also because the sociological divisions within them did not become ironclad, built on a foundation of complexion. Do I mean, then, that Hispanic Caribbean slaves never experienced creolization? They did not experience it when those islands first made attempts at being plantation colonies, because those attempts were so weak and intermittent. Nor did they, as I see it, in the course of the next two centuries.[13]

Thus in the 1750s and later, those three Hispanic societies certainly did not look the way the northern European sugar colonies had looked a century earlier. It seems quite certain that no creole language arose in Cuba or Puerto Rico, while the Dominican Republic did not have a sugar revival in the eighteenth century. We also know that by 1775, these Hispanic societies had become entirely different from the non-Hispanic plantation islands because they already had large populations of people of color, many of whom were free, at least some of whom were of intermediate social status—and all of whom spoke Spanish.[14] The absence of a creole language is a coefficient of these other differences.

While I have set the emergence of a creole language as a sort of sine qua non for the creolization process, this condition does not tell us what else was happening culturally in these societies. The three Hispanic cases—Cuba, Puerto Rico, and Santo Domingo—developed in radically different directions after the 1760s. Cuba would become an enormous and hugely profitable plantation colony. But by 1820, the slave trade had come under political pressure from Great Britain, bent on stopping the trade. Puerto Rico wanted to do as Cuba had done, by buying slaves; and later by acquiring those who were smuggled in. Its plantation sector, particularly in the south of the island, tried valiantly, but being smaller, poorer, and lacking "clout," was less successful than Cuba's.[15]

Yet while these three societies eventually went in rather different directions from each other by virtue of their previous histories, none went the way of the rest of the plantation Caribbean. There may be grounds for doubting that these were solidly homogeneous societies. But they certainly stand largely stand apart from the rest of the region because of their different histories, both "racial" and demographic.

In spite of an abundance of solid research, our comparative grasp of Caribbean history remains fragmentary. The comparative study of Caribbean peasantries remains in its infancy; and contrasts between the Hispanic and non-Hispanic cases could be fruitful. In the Greater Antilles, large Caucasian rural agricultural populations arose only in the Hispanic cases. Black-white ratios were important in the relationships between peasants and plantation workers in these societies, and those relationships evolved differentially, even in recent Caribbean history.

Looking back further, we see in the Hispanic cases in particular the need to grasp more firmly the variant connections between race and rural life and labor. Francisco Scarano, for example (1989), has stressed our need to understand much better what the relations between free workers and slaves were like in Puerto Rico, even in slavery times, as planters debated on the one hand whether to push for more slaves and on the other how best to exact labor from their white and mixed-race—but free—fellow citizens. The differing fates of island peoples, as plantation economies rose and fell, was apparent to Herman Merivale, the British student of colonies, writing in 1830. Merivale deplored the rise of plantation slavery in Puerto Rico in the 1830s, just as Jamaica was approaching the emancipation of its slaves: "The tropical colonies of Spain were commonwealths in an epoch when those of most other nations were mere factories; they are now rapidly acquiring the degrading characteristics of factories, while ours, we may hope, are advancing toward the dignity of commonwealths" (1967:41). Merivale's optimism about British colonialism was wildly excessive, if he had the welfare of Jamaica's slaves in mind. Yet he pointed to an illuminating contrast. Hispanic Caribbean economic exceptionalism merits much more careful reflection than I can provide here. But I would argue, nonetheless, for a much more comparative look at the Caribbean region.

I do not offer these materials in order to hazard a new interpretation of Caribbean history but to suggest instead that a good deal of that history still remains partly concealed from us. I find it striking that the history of all three Hispanic colonies diverged sharply from the histories of the other islands; that they developed so differently in their demography; and that their people perceive themselves today and are perceived as Hispanic in tradition—in ways that differ sharply, I believe, from the ways in which Jamaicans, say, or Kittsians or Martiniquans conceive of their identities. I grant that this is an inexact and underexplained assertion. Further comparative historical research will probably unearth other differences that matter more to our understanding of these places. Good history—careful, "longitudinal" (carried on over lengthy periods, dealing with lengthy periods, with room for corrections and additions), and always open to new interpretations—is essential to do this.

I had viewed the Hispanic islands—Cuba, eastern Santo Domingo, and Puero Rico—as distinctive because they had not developed classic plantation economies. But I had failed to make explicit that it took a certain kind of plantation frenzy to open the way for what I define here as creolization. In the Hispanic colonies, without creolization, a quite different sort of society was able to take shape and to grow. I have tried here to make more visible the differences between the Hispanic and the non-Hispanic societies.

Notes

References

Index

Notes

1. Caribbean Anthropology and History

1. There are excellent grounds for wondering, for example, whether an official racism is a necessary accompaniment to fascism. The question would have been pointed even in the 1930s, when some state fascisms such as the Italian—at least at home—were less racist in outlook than some democracies, such as the United States. A multiracial fascism would spare its leaders much wasted time and economic resources—as some nations seem now to have grasped at last.

2. Skaggs's (1994) excellent history of the frantic U.S. search for islands with guano deposits, a strange episode in the history of American imperialism, should not be omitted from any study of the United States in the Caribbean. As part of the guano craze, the Haitian island of Navassa was simply seized by the United States, on the basis of a congressional definition of what constituted legal territorial seizure. A tragic drama unfolded on Navassa and in the Baltimore courts, involving black freed persons. It is ably recounted by Skaggs.

3. There are now genealogical sources for Haiti (Saint Domingue) available online. Quite possibly more could be learned by historical research about Alexander Du Bois and his Haitian kinfolk than was possible in 1993, when Lewis's book was published.

4. In later years, one of his closest assistants was Bahamian. He was also a friend of the Trinidadian physician John Alcindor, who practiced in London.

5. This realization is signaled most dramatically when Du Bois writes of Franz Boas's commencement address at Atlanta University. "Franz Boas came to Atlanta University where I was teaching history in 1906 and said to a graduating class: You need not be ashamed of your African past: and then he recounted the history of black kingdoms south of the Sahara for a thousand years. I was too astonished to speak. All of this I had never heard and I came then to real-

ize how the silence and neglect of science can let truth utterly disappear or even be unconsciously distorted" (Du Bois 1939:vii).

6. Geggus (1997:31), in an incisive and illuminating overview of Caribbean resistance in the period 1789–1815, writes: "Slaves in the nineteenth century knew slavery was under attack; they were exposed to the growing European preoccupation with individual liberty; and the searing drama of Saint Domingue had demonstrated to them and their owners, the possibility of successful revolt." Julius Scott's pioneering unpublished thesis (1986) on the global repercussions of this revolution broke new ground when it was written. See his essay in Dubois and Scott 2009.

7. The large islands and the small had somewhat different colonial pasts. Spain occupied the four largest islands in the early 1500s, and ruled unchallenged for 125 years. Indigenous Carib people lived in the small island chain, and stoutly resisted the Europeans. They were mostly left alone for an additional century. By 1625, however, Spain's rivals began to occupy the small islands and to challenge Spain on the large ones.

8. McNeill and McNeill (2003) have written a fine global historical overview. Wallerstein's (2004) admirable statement of his own world system theory is must reading, as is Wolf's (1982) wonderful study of the relationship of Europe to the outside world. Marx's *Capital* is remarkable for its anticipation of, and profound effect upon, later thought.

9. Cuba and Puerto Rico. What had been the Spanish colony of Santo Domingo, the eastern two-thirds of Hispaniola, established its independence in 1844 by breaking away from Haiti, which had occupied and controlled the colony intermittently after 1804.

10. Tea *(Camellia sinensis)* was a major exception at the time, its history in the West closely tied to Great Britain, China, the domination of India, and the Opium Wars.

11. There have been several different approaches to the modernizing effects of enslavement and plantations. James proposes that the specific life conditions created for the slaves on the sugar plantations produced social and psychological changes analogous to those of the Industrial Revolution on European society at a later point in history. Shilliam (2008) argues that slavery produced a modernity wholly divorced from the European experience. Beckles (1998) also writes about modernity and Caribbean slavery, but is more concerned with the concept of freedom in Western thought, expressed most powerfully by Patterson (1982), that the West's conception of freedom was a coefficient of the reality of slavery. My view seeks to assess what the complex of slavery,

sugar, and the plantation did each day to the lives and the personalities of the slaves.

12. Eltis and Richardson give 1,013,068 for Jamaica, and 772,734 for Saint Domingue.

13. *New Yorker* writer Joseph Mitchell often wrote about people who were neither rich nor important. In an author's note to his collection *McSorley's Wonderful Saloon* (1943), he refers to a fashion at the time among some writers to call such people "little." "I regard this phrase as patronizing and repulsive," he wrote. "There are no little people in this book. They are as big as you are, whoever you are."

14. My teacher, Ruth Benedict (1948:592), stressed the value of such work in her presidential address to the American Anthropological Association.

15. Intermixture between European and other populations varied over time, and led in some islands to large populations of genetically and culturally "mixed" peoples.

16. We have no photographs of them. But we know that a preponderant proportion of the Puerto Rican people carry genes from these different populations.

17. In the British colony of Barbados and in early British Jamaica, indentured servants and kidnapped and deported Britons and Irishmen briefly worked alongside African slaves.

18. David Brion Davis (2003:29–33) has described how American unwillingness to recognize the absolutely central role of slavery and African Americans in the building of the American republic, and the societal debt that it represents, would lead to the terrible—still vigorous—national misperception that "if it had not been for the Negro," a New World Paradise would have been ours to perfect. This is our classic national example of blaming the victim.

19. Laurent Dubois's history of slavery and emancipation in French Guadeloupe (2004) is a poignant examination in that case of what Orlando Patterson refers to in his book *An Absence of Ruins* (1967).

20. I mentioned earlier that many anthropologists have no interest in the historical. But in recent years anthropologists like the late John Murra, and scholars such as Stephan Palmié, Jerome Handler, and Richard Price, often do work not so readily distinguished from that being done by historians such as Fredrick Cooper, Rebecca Scott, Laurent Dubois, or Thomas Holt.

21. No longer (if ever) a justified claim—historians usually know the written language they need and speak it as well as the anthropologists, if it is a written language.

22. I suppose that there may be some personality traits that, in the aggregate, tend to distinguish persons who become anthropologists from those who become historians. But I wouldn't bet on it.

23. The Bahamas are not usually considered part of the Caribbean. While it is true that the people who were already living there already knew where they were, Columbus *did* discover the New World, as far as the West is concerned.

24. From 1833–1834 until 1838 in the British West Indies, people were neither free nor slaves but "apprentices." In many ways, particularly in their treatment, it was mostly as if they were still enslaved.

25. The classic case was Barbados, Britain's first Caribbean colony. Though it began with British settlement and small-scale farm production, the success of sugar plantations based on slavery was swift and thorough. The small farmers were driven out and never returned. Much the same happened in other Caribbean locales.

26. Slavery is of course ancient. But the slavery of agricultural commodity mass production, an "industrial" slavery, was perfected in the New World. In Europe, little like it could be found outside the medieval galleys and their press gangs.

27. The idea of "frontier" is credited mainly to the work of American historian Frederick Jackson Turner and his epigones. For a contrasting view as to whose work was the fundamental basis for frontier history, see Benson (1950).

28. The difference is significant. While most plantations were located in the tropics, the plantation form is found elsewhere. Thompson demonstrated that the driving force is expanding world capitalism. Where a frontier facilitates the use of cheap land, labor is likely to be coerced or enslaved, and the plantation form will flourish without regard to latitude.

29. The history of plantations, particularly in their association with regions of the erstwhile colonial world, has been one of terrible environmental destruction. It is no accident that the German term for plantation farming is *Raubbau*, or "robber agriculture." Forests, water, animal and plant life, and the soil itself were sacrificed repeatedly to garner quick profits. Watts (1987) has done a solid job of describing those consequences, especially for the British West Indies. Recently, Funes Monzote (2008) has produced an exacting and thorough historical account of the destruction of the Cuban landscape by plantation development. Hollander (2008) provides a penetrating overview of the Florida sugarcane industry and its depressing economic, social and environmental consequences for the Everglades.

30. The most important urban concentrations in the insular Caribbean continue to be situated in the Hispanic islands, particularly Cuba and Puerto Rico.

Longtime early European settlement and deferred plantation eras made a different kind of city possible on those islands.

31. What did not emerge in those pioneering centuries were bandit leaders or warlords of the sort familiar from European and Asian history, and the reason is obvious—there simply was not enough population yet in these frontier societies to be preyed on.

32. Now there are five; in Puerto Rico, the Hispanic colonial past is distinguishable from what the United States has brought.

33. Making use of a far broader perspective than I do, Cooper (2005) has taken very good aim at this rhetoric.

2. Jamaica

1. Of course it was a black and white and "red" (Amerindian) Atlantic. Chromatic categories serve a purpose if they make us remember at least that it was not a white Atlantic. They are, however, markedly ahistorical and geographically inexact, for the Caribbean.

2. None was consumed sweetened by its inventors in the locus of origin— neither tea (China), nor coffee (Yemen) nor chocolate (Mexico). It is perhaps worth mentioning that chocolate did not become a commercially practical solid confection until the late nineteenth century.

3. I do not mean to exaggerate the limitations against which free colored Jamaicans struggled. Papers by Higman, Shepherd and Monteith, and Smith, for example (in Shepherd 2002) document their modest but real economic achievements, in penkeeping, on coffee estates, and otherwise. But these people would never win the wealth or political power displayed in the eighteenth century by the free colored of prerevolutionary Saint Domingue.

4. Higman mentions Lady Nugent's famous book of her adventures as wife of the governor of Jamaica. A guest of aged bachelor planter Simon Taylor at his Golden Grove estate, Lady Nugent reports that she was told that Taylor "had a numerous family some almost on every one of his estates" (Higman 2005:143). Taylor was not exceptional. Mathieson (1926:59), a careful historian, writes of Jamaica: "Relations with coloured women were all but universal; even the married planter had often a mixed family of whites and browns." Thoughtful readers will reflect on the effects of this almost universal practice by the society's governing class upon the moral outlook of the society as a whole.

5. An anecdote from the school desegregation period in the U.S. South has it that a town hall janitor in a small southern town overheard angered councilmen

declaring their opposition to desegregation. One said "Whatever happens, I do not want to see our children going to school with their children!" And the janitor supposedly piped up: "You mean you don't want to see *our* children going to school with *your* children! Some of *your* children have been going to school with *our* children for a mighty long time!"

6. Jamaica was not the only slave society in which concubinage was so common as to be almost institutionalized; many children were born as slaves from such unions in all slave societies. But in some, more fathers freed their children and married their mothers, as in French Saint Domingue. The implications of this different mating pattern are sociologically very weighty, but we have no statistics to help us.

7. A thoughtful and illuminating description of the plantation's occupational work categories, based on the slave lists, comes from Craton and Walvin's study of Worthy Park plantation (1970).

8. The figures are admittedly unreliable. These are Brathwaite's (1971:168) for Jamaica in 1820. The slave population of Jamaica was nearly half that in all the British West Indian colonies. Higman (1984) has been particularly careful; he calculates that in 1834, Jamaica slaves totalled 311,070 (Higman 1984:74); whites 16,000; and freed persons (of all colors) 42,000 (see also Higman 1976:142, 298).

9. Built into the complicated Jamaican social system was an odd formula—similar to that in all Anglo-Caribbean colonies—by which a tiny minority of people of part-African ancestry could become, over time, legally white. The number of such persons was socially inconsequential, but the formula is theoretically interesting. Brathwaite 2005:167 discusses persons who became legally white by genealogical narrowing. Tambiah (1985:212–251), analyzing hypergamy and caste in south India, uncovered surprising structural parallels to the "whitening process" in Jamaica but has never written about this specifically.

10. Though I cannot do justice to the social and political history of color in either Jamaica or Haiti, I must address some of the issues to which that history was related. In both prerevolutionary Saint Domingue and Jamaica, sharp attention was paid both to physical appearance and to civil status. But I argue that the outcome of the growth of a free group of persons, intermediate in appearance, and in some instances having property and influence, took radically different forms in these two societies.

11. In 1780–87, between 15,000 and 24,000 Jamaican slaves died of hunger, mostly because the North American food trade was disrupted by the American Revolution (Sheridan 1973:632; Brathwaite 2005) and hurricane damage.

12. Burnard (2004:143) points out how slave marketing, though eventually threatening to the plantation system, was also recognized by the planters themselves as *necessary*. Most difficult for the slaves was securing adequate protein, especially animal protein. Though they were supposed to be given a ration of animal food, it was commonly unfit to eat—rotten, or consisting mostly of bones and tendons. Rats were commonly caught and eaten; fishing was very important (Price 1966); and of course meat and other food was stolen at times. In a penetrating article (1988), Lichtenstein shows convincingly that stealing by slaves was often an act of resistance, not simply a lack of morality. Slaves recognized that their labor was being steadily stolen from them.

13. Thanks to Prof. Rebecca Scott for pointing this out.

14. I do not mean to exaggerate the importance of these slaves' holdings for slave nutrition—their benefit was limited. Yet their existence and their sociological effects raise questions about how the total system operated, and where slaves learned what they needed to know. Since I first wrote on the significance of independent, nondirected agricultural production (1961) and commercial marketing (1955) *by slaves,* subsequent studies have shown that such activities were common throughout Afro-America. These activities provide important evidence that the slaves had by no means failed to learn the basic lessons of capitalist individualism, even though their failure was widely proclaimed. (See, e.g. Gaspar 1998; Beckles 1991; Berlin and Morgan 1991, 1993; Morgan 1998.)

15. Just as every parade once had to have its Moor, so every justification of state violence must have its intellectuals.

16. This critical event in Jamaica's political, economic, and even racial history has received considerable attention in the literature (e.g. Hall 1992; Heuman 1981, 1994; Holt 1992). Heuman 1994 begins with a brief but useful review of such studies.

17. Some were not plantation colonies, or only barely, and what happened in those cases was clearly different (Mathieson 1926:245–255).

18. Hochschild 2005:347.

19. I deal here only in passing with the Apprenticeship—surely one of the most abusive "transitions" ever visited on defenseless people in history (see, e.g., Paton 2001).

20. Thomas Carlyle's "Essay on the Nigger Question" captures planter sentiment perfectly, right down to its title when republished.

21. Sligoville, named after the ex-governor the Marquis of Sligo, was actually founded before August 1, 1838. It was the only such case.

22. Once Apprenticeship ended, it was not possible to work freed people with the total contempt for their welfare or safety that slavery had made possible. Adamson (1972) has shown that on the very day freedom came, the establishment of even minimum treatment standards for free laborers in British Guiana meant that 13,000 more workers were needed there,

23. Two fine essays by Catherine Hall (1992:205–295) capture much of the missionary "mindset" as well as the temper of the times in nineteenth-century Jamaica. In a later essay (1993) she sets the free village movement in a wide historical canvas that includes both Jamaica and Great Britain.

24. The word "pen," used in Jamaica, is about the same as "farm." The "pimento" is allspice, an evergreen tree crop *(Pimenta dioica)*.

25. Though for clear historical reasons, only a minority of the peasants in the Hispanic locales, Puerto Rico, Cuba, and the Dominican Republic, seem to be African American.

26. I once told Hlaw Myint, an eminent Burmese economist, that I was impressed when I had learned that two of the world's most interesting development economists, Sir W. Arthur Lewis (who was St. Lucian) and Hlaw Myint himself, had come from peasant countries. He laughed. "Ah," he said, "but unlike Arthur, I come from a real peasant country!"

27. Dumping cheap food in Caribbean societies and calling it "aid" has provided textbook examples of how to wean peasantries from their love of the land.

28. I mean to say they would realize he was colored even if he was *publicly* white, and no one would ever say anything about it—publicly.

29. Such awakenings were frequent in my Caribbean fieldwork. Travel may be broadening; happily, it occasionally can teach some humility.

30. I still remember seeing a man being pursued by angry peasants in Haiti. He had been caught stealing food out of the ground. I realized to my horror that they fully intended to stone him to death. Luckily, he escaped. I never found out what finally happened in the shooting case, but there is no evidence that the pen-keeper ever went to jail. (Thanks to Frances Salmon and Celia Brown for their efforts to help me pin down more details.)

31. I have mentioned that James Williams, the apprentice whose testimony was made famous by Sturge and probably hastened the end of Apprenticeship, came from a property very near Angwin Crawle, out of which Sturge Town was founded. A Land Settlement scheme begun in the 1930s and enlarged after World War II had made a little additional land available in Knapdale, next to Sturge Town.

32. It need hardly be said that all of these skills have been in vertiginous decline during the last half century.

3. Haiti

1. There is now a fine English-language scholarly literature on Haiti, which complements the French-language historiography. See for example Geggus 1982, 1983, 2002; Fick 1990; Dubois 2004; Garrigus 2006; Dubois and Garrigus 2006; Bell 2007. In this book, Haitian words are written in McConnell-Laubach orthography. See McConnell (1957).

2. Perhaps we should except from this heady claim at least the "precious metal" conquests of the Spaniards in Mexico and the Andes.

3. Napoléon 1858–70:7:640–642.

4. A biography that admirably captures the uncertainties, by the writer Madison Smartt Bell (2007), probably does almost all that can be done with what is known—plus some guesses—about Louverture. Serious students of Louverture will benefit from a reading of Geggus's subtle and penetrating essay, "'The *volte-face*' of Toussaint Louverture," in Geggus (2002).

5. I know of no more convincing portrait of Louverture and his dilemma in this period than Laurent Dubois (2004:231–250).

6. That story is probably apocryphal. But the buttons from the jacket Toussaint wore in prison made their way by a circuitous route to the Cooper-Hewitt Museum in New York City, where they can still be seen. Each is an exquisite reproduction of scenes painted by Agostino Brunias in Saint Domingue (Geracimos 2000). The accession number for those eighteen buttons is 1949–49–1/18. My thanks to Sarah Coffin for her help.

7. The name *haïti* is said to be an aboriginal (Taino) term meaning "mountainous" or "mountainous land." Haiti marked its two hundredth anniversary—unremarked everywhere and by everyone except the Haitians—on January 1, 2004.

8. Laurent Dubois (2004:301) entitles his account of that revolution—surely the best account available—*Avengers of the New World*. He quotes Dessalines: "I have saved my country. I have avenged America."

9. "How is it that we hear the loudest yelps for liberty among the drivers of negroes?" (Samuel Johnson 1775:93–144).

10. Though these were obviously not the only New World countries with legal slavery.

11. The Haitian revolutionaries provided some record of their political vision, much of it understandably dark. There is, for example, the vengeful and violent

Declaration of Independence, commissioned by General Jean Jacques Dessalines and first read in public on January 1, 1804 (Dubois and Garrigus 2006:188–191). Primary sources include many of Toussaint's letters, his so-called dictatorial proclamation of 1801, several of the Haitian constitutions, and other materials.

All the same, in order meaningfully to try to contrast the aims of these two revolutionary movements, American and Haitian, we would have to take into account important background facts, including the education and outlooks of their respective leaders. To have expected the Haitian rebels to think about (let alone to write about) a society built on political ideas drawn from the European Enlightenment would be entirely disingenuous.

12. An ironical aside. Jean Baptiste Donatien de Vimeur, Comte de Rochambeau, fought on the side of Washington at Yorktown, and was thanked by the revolutionary congress. His son, Donatien Marie Joseph de Vimeur, Vicomte de Rochambeau, fought there as well, under his father. But the son went on to fight against the slaves in Saint Domingue, where he was distinguished for his cruelty. He was captured by the British in Samana in 1803, fleeing Dessalines, and was not freed until 1811.

13. "Damn sugar, damn coffee, damn colonies!" Napoleon is said to have exclaimed, after Leclerc's death. He eventually sold those 565 million acres for the princely sum of $US 15,000,000. See Kukla 2003.

14. McClellan's (1992) study of colonial Saint Domingue shows that science flourished there, especially in the urban centers. But like nearly all else, it was because of the rich and free that it was there at all.

15. Being two or more generations away from slavery came to be an important index of status. Though it was not made into a legal device in Saint Domingue, many people of color cherished the idea. The term *affranchi*—freedperson—was disliked by many of the *gens de couleur* because it misrepresented their genealogical distance from their free French ancestors.

16. For a corrective to excessive enthusiasm over the more humane aspects of the Code Noir, see Dayan 1995.

17. The history of Caribbean slave societies is no basis on which to assert that any society composed of two populations, widely differing in culture and in power, will inevitably create some kind of intermediate group (or groups). But it certainly happened over and over again in the islands. The Saint Domingue case is arresting because its revolution would have taken on a different form had it not been for the free colored and their role in the changing relations of revolutionary France to the planters of Saint Domingue.

18. Fick (1997:56, 2000:12) cites the generally accepted figures; in 1789 there were 30,000 whites and 28,000 *gens de couleur,* or free people of color.

19. In an introduction to the Haitian Revolution, Geggus (2002:10) writes: "In general . . . free people of color acted like the slave-owners they usually were, and were careful not to have their cause confused with that of the black masses."

20. I know of no evidence that white Jamaican planters ever feared being mistaken for free colored by Englishmen in London. The social situation in Saint Domingue seems to have been quite different from that in Jamaica.

21. She wisely adds (72): "More research still needs to be done to determine what proportion of the roughly 28,000 free coloreds of Saint Domingue owned 30 percent of the plantations and one-quarter of the slaves."

22. Leyburn (1966:16) writes: "The 28,000 *gens de couleur* included all free persons who had African blood in their veins [*sic*]. It is highly probable that without this third group, there would have been no violent outbreak in 1791, no achievement of final independence in 1804, and no such caste system as exists in Haiti at the present time."

23. Heuman's (1981) thoughtful history of the free coloreds in Jamaica mostly concentrates on their political evolution. He tabulates estimates for free colored: 10,000 (free colored and free black) in 1789; 28,800 and 10,000 in 1825; and 31,000 and 11,000 in 1834. Brathwaite's classic study deals with the free colored but does not fully review their economic status.

24. In effect, the Jamaican planters followed the so-called one-drop rule and from the first aimed to regulate by law the fate of those phenotypically identifiable as "not white." Fourth-generation descendants of a black-white cross who had been lineally "whitened" in each generation were considered white. But it is clear that the number of such persons in Jamaica was always small. People of color nonetheless sought to be granted some of the rights they were denied on grounds of race. Those rights were rarely conceded.

25. We Americans do not realize how astonishingly silly we may appear in our preoccupations with the pedigree of the late Senator Thurmond's daughter by his family's maid or the genealogical complications of founding father Thomas Jefferson. We should be much more aware of how *commonplace* such matters were, in societies inhabited by masters and slaves.

26. Deerr's chart (1949:1:240) shows clayed (semirefined, whitened) sugar down to one ton in 1820, but Haiti still produced 1,212 tons of moscovado in that year. Its production continued to fall thereafter. Deerr provides a photo of a Haitian mill (facing 234) dated to 1830 that was not animal powered, but gives no explanation.

27. German and Swiss interests in the late nineteenth century eventuated in the development of a prosperous resident German-Haitian community, which

the United States found menacing before World War I. The U.S. occupation of Haiti in 1915 was an effort in part to forestall the country's becoming a coaling station for the German fleet.

28. When I worked in Haiti in 1958, the Haitian expression for "shank's mare" was "M té vini sou dè vityèlo mwê" (I came on my own two feet—*vityèlo* having coming from the name of a Corsican shoemaker who taught so many Haitians how to make shoes that his surname came to mean "shoe.") Half a century ago it was still easy to find in Haiti forges, sugar mills, and tanneries hardly changed from those typical of the seventeenth century.

29. Much is made of the quixotic succession of illegitimate military governments under which Haiti has suffered. But the Haitian countryside was for most of the time tranquil, even remote from politics.

    Sheller's (2000) fascinating historical study of Haiti and Jamaica compares the rights of the ex-slaves in postemancipation Jamaica and postrevolutionary Haiti. She brings three kinds of rights—economic, social, and political—into play and suggests that some students (this writer among them) have exaggerated the political passivity of the Haitian peasantry. I think lack of organization and of institutions hamstrung the Haitian peasantry. Jamaica after slavery was still a colony and politically still dominated by planters. Jamaica had institutions that reached all parts of the countryside and, as Holt stresses, there had been a brief period when politics escaped racial categories. Political responsiveness there could take advantage of existing institutions. In contrast, the prerevolutionary infrastructure of Saint Domingue was meant primarily for the elite. It had been nearly erased by the Revolution. The only Haitian postrevolutionary *national* institution that reached the countryside was the military. It was no help at all when it came to the political rights of the peasantry.

30. The leading opponent of the campaign was the novelist and poet Jacques Roumain, who was also a founder of the Haitian Communist Party. He was exiled by the Haitian government for his troublesomeness. His paper (1944) on the campaign against "voodoo" still makes good reading.

31. The United States established a very creditable school of agronomy and extension service during the occupation. By the time of my first fieldwork, though (1958–1959), it was poorly funded and hardly functioning.

32. Many Haitian families have French and German ties, some going back to the postrevolutionary, nineteenth-century continuation of coffee production and trade by the peasantry, after the total destruction of the sugar plantations.

33. There is a long historical record for this place, and the southern peninsula had its own role to play in Haitian history (Garrigus 2006); but I cannot address that here.

34. The terminology for market women is large and quite precise. The terms are not synonyms; they stand for differing categories of intermediary.

35. *Komè*: co-godmother. As was often true in Latin America, godparenthood was a very serious institution, but the terms were often used as casual terms of address, too—like "brother" or "Pop" in the United States.

36. Each market woman carries her money in a tiny cloth sack (Cr. *sakit*) she wears around her neck under her dress. In it there are invariably sesame seeds (Cr. *rôrôli*) to protect the money (Métraux 1951). Clever thieves, called *aousa*, are able to use bewitched coins to wish the money out of the seller's *sakit*. The term *aousa* may come from the name Hausa.

4. Puerto Rico

1. This is not the place to discuss Spain's imperial policy overseas. But the society that reconquered much of the Hispanic peninsula, winning back Catholic Spain from its Muslim rulers, was not prepared in 1492 to become a commercial, capitalist, and entrepreneurial power. It was centuries before Spain would "catch up" to her northern European adversaries.

2. Important essays on the early history of sugar in the Hispano-Caribbean—Rodríguez Morel for Santo Domingo and De la Fuente for Cuba—appear in Schwartz (2004). His own introduction to the book is one of the best essays on New World sugar in the literature.

3. Even before the Americans arrived, though, there were some entirely modern plantations on the island (Ramos Mattei 1985, 1988). With the U.S. occupation, technical modernization became island-wide.

4. The so-called one-drop rule that became characteristic of the U.S. racial code is absent in Puerto Rico. This, too, has meaning for the larger story.

5. Even so, in 1531, for which we have one of the few precise figures available for so early a period, the "African" population of the island amounted to 2,264, a majority—of whom 85 percent were living in the capital city, San Juan (Picó 2006:47).

6. Sugar did remain the biggest money-earner in the official (legal) trade to Seville and Cádiz during 1550–1650 (Picó 2006:54)—more a measure of Puerto Rico's isolation, perhaps, than of sugar's importance there.

7. Before about 1800, these rural folk seem not to have been really under the control of the island's central government. "Peasants," writes Wolf (1966:3–4),

"are rural cultivators whose surpluses are transferred to a dominant group of rulers that uses the surpluses both to underwrite its own standard of living and to distribute the remainder to groups in society that do not farm but must be fed for their specific goods and services in turn."

8. There is no comparable population in Jamaican history except a band of maroons the Spaniards left behind. In the history of Santo Domingo, the buccaneers *(boucaniers)* who fed off feral cattle and harassed the Spanish colonists in the west of the island might have become similar, until they were driven off. Puerto Ricans sometimes incant the phrase "Que no es ynga es mandinga"— meaning essentially "If one has no Amerindian ancestry, one will have some African ancestry." No one, that is, can be sure of being only white. Though merely a *refrán* or saying, in Puerto Rico this seems to be in some accord with history.

9. Admittedly, what happened to legally freed people under the Apprenticeship in the British West Indies and a few comparable schemes elsewhere much resembled events in Puerto Rico, but those cases were supposedly to ease the transition from *slavery*. Whites were not affected by them. See, e.g., Knox 1977; Mintz 1979.

10. Scarano writes: "Slave labor in sugar was preponderant in Puerto Rico up to 1850 and probably represented *about half of the labor input* in the industry in the years immediately preceding abolition in 1873" (1984:xxii; italics added). He is referring here to the Ponce sugar plantations in particular.

11. What Dutch sociologist Harry Hoetink (1967) referred to as the "suppleness" of race relations in the Hispanic Antilles is probably connected to just such deviations from the social patterns of more typical plantation societies, such as Jamaica.

12. I do hope it will not be thought that I am saying Puerto Rico was not a racist society. But it differs in its attitudes. I saw labor leaders arguing in favor of working people and referring to themselves as *nosotros los negritos*—though many of them were phenotypically white.

13. A larger number of African *phenotypes* is the result of *qualitatively* different (genetic) processes from those resulting in the presence of any African *cultural* materials. There is no connection between culture materials and the genetic origins of those who may (or may not) perpetuate them.

14. That sugar hacienda had been owned at the turn of the century by one Dn. Pastor Díaz, a famed local figure, who was still well remembered half a century later. The chimney itself was a local landmark, referred to when I worked there as "la chimenea de Dn. Pastor."

15. Puerto Rico has been called a territory, a dependency, a commonwealth, and other things. As far as certain basic political and economic facts are concerned, it is a colony.

16. Since my work in the south coast, a fine monograph by Figueroa (2005) on the history of sugar and slavery especially in nineteenth-century Guayama, has appeared.

17. Giusti-Cordero's dissertation (1994), a historical-anthropological study of a Puerto Rican community, provides the single best critique of ideal-type abstractions such as "rural proletarian" and "peasant" in the social science literature.

18. Figueroa (2005) discusses the struggle (mostly losing) waged by the newly freed in Guayama to establish themselves as peasants. Black peasantries arose throughout the British West Indies, but meagerly, if at all, in the Hispanic Caribbean. The work of Rebecca Scott (1985, 2001, 2005) is particularly important in this connection.

19. It was a standing joke that Jauca people only went to church after they had died, because they had to pass the church to get to the cemetery, on the other side of the town. I saw it with my own eyes, when José "Gueni" Godineaux died. His coffin was carried to town, a brief service was held in the church, and the funeral party then trudged on with his coffin to the cemetery.

20. It was, however, becoming common (c. 1950) for the girl's family to "denounce" *(denunciar)* the male partner in court, in order to pin down his legal obligation to support any children. The growing outmigration of young males spurred this practice.

21. Juan Giusti-Cordero has suggested to me that this practice, intended or not, was a clear rejection of outside authority, both civil and religious. He asks— and I do not know—whether a like pattern can be documented for Cuba or the Dominican Republic.

22. I strongly endorse Kroeber's assertion (1948: 255) that "a cultural fact is always a historical fact; and its most immediate understanding, and usually the fullest understanding of it to which we can attain, is a historical one."

23. It comes from a suggestion of Juan Giusti-Cordero.

24. See Weisskopf (1985) for a sharp look at "development" in Puerto Rico in the 1980s.

25. I think the one-drop rule had begun to penetrate Puerto Rican perception in the 1990s. The vast nonwhite immigration to the United States since the 1960s may be weakening that "rule" here. It is conceivable that as the United States becomes more flexible in these regards, Puerto Rico may become slightly less so.

26. All of this to be treated with the reader's skepticism.

27. "¡María!" "¿Sí, Señor?" "María, dígame, Don Pedro—es negro?" "Don Pedro? Sí, Señor, es negro." "Pero María, piénsalo bien, Don Pedro—es negro *negro?*" Ella piensa, y entonces dice, muy cuidadosamente: "Sí, Señor—Don Pedro es negro negro." Y el contesta: "Pues, María, escúchame bien—Don Pedro—es negro negro *negro?*" Y entonces dice ella: "*Ah, no,* Señor, negro negro negro, no!"

28. Or Negro, or colored, or Afro-American, or African American, or oddest of all, "minorities."

29. Not to mention, especially in the U.S. South, being accustomed to people who may look slightly negroid to an outsider but define themselves behaviorally and *are treated by local whites* as white.

30. Though more commonly they are between people of approximately the same "color." The preference for a wife who is lighter in color, once widespread in the African-American middle class, seems much less important to Puerto Ricans. It seems to me—impressionistically only—much more important in Jamaica and in Haiti.

5. Creolization, Culture, and Social Institutions

1. Depending, I suppose, on one's age and on how enthusiastically one embraces opinions that are now increasingly sold as eternal verities, the idea of a single coherent movement toward global economic oneness may have seemed enormously appealing in recent years. If one remembered other such enthusiasms in the past, however, then considerable restraint would have been appropriate. Events are now proving as much.

2. I refer again to the work of Edgar Thompson (1932), who stressed the political and frontier nature of plantation societies, in reaction to the habit of defining them primarily in geographical terms as "tropical."

3. Brathwaite (2005) is one of the first and best works to develop the idea of creolization with a Caribbean historical example. My own stress is on the role played by the slaves themselves in creating a creolized society.

4. In the Hispanic Antilles—which means all of the islands for the first 125 years—some native peoples were enslaved, and great numbers died through war, disease, and maltreatment. But sugar plantation development was spotty and uneven before the second half of the eighteenth century, in those Caribbean colonies that remained Spanish.

5. Summary facts can be misleading. But for my purposes here, I mean Jamaica 1655–1838; Saint Domingue 1697–1804; and Puerto Rico 1510–1876.

6. A few scholars have argued forcefully that some groups of ethnically homogeneous slaves reached the Americas and were able to perpetuate cultural materials substantially unchanged. That did happen in some cases. Such exceptions do not invalidate the general point I am making here.

7. I am not a linguist. But I think the sociological questions raised by these languages do not have linguistic answers only.

8. I mean here, of course, those that are spoken in the New World.

9. I used the term "institution" earlier in two different senses, meaning a group that meets regularly enough, and with enough motivation, to develop its own internal order; and also meaning the rules (e.g., for courtship) that are invoked to guarantee regularity and order. My goal throughout is explanation. The seeming inconsistency results from my seeking to avoid a lengthy theoretical discussion.

10. Recent research, particularly in Brazil (Nishida 2003; Matory 2005; and the essays by Alpers, Parés, Kiddy, and Kriger in Curto and Soulodre-La France 2005) shows that the concept of institution is now being incorporated into analyses of what happened to enslaved Africans and their descendants in the Americas.

11. Much could be added here. But it is not the place to debate chimpomats and talking dolphins; even less to lay an axe to ideologically motivated theories of social evolution; or to review (yet again) the unremarkable truism/discovery that one culture is not equal to one society is not equal to one language. I leave those tasks to the next generation (or possibly to the last).

12. Scarano (1984) demonstrates that when Spain, under British pressure after 1808, agreed to stop the slave trade, Puerto Rico continued to receive smuggled slaves until at least the 1830s, but in declining numbers.

13. The Cuban plantation system based on slavery, post-1762, grew astonishingly and quite dwarfed what happened analogously in Puerto Rico. See, for example, Moreno Fraginals and Traviesas, (1978). On the nature of creolization, see among others Palmié 2007a, 2007b; Eriksen 2007.

14. Santo Domingo, the third Hispanic "sister," followed a different path. Its plantations developed mainly under North American tutelage, in the twentieth century.

15. Those differences had sequelae of their own. Unlike Puerto Rico, both Cuba and Santo Domingo were marked by terrible racial "incidents"—the so-called insurrection in Cuba (1912) and the massacres of Dominicans of Haitian origin in Santo Domingo in 1937. These events were related to issues of national identity and labor, but I cannot look at them more closely here.

References

Adamson, Alan H. 1972. *Sugar without Slaves: The Political Economy of British Guiana, 1838–1904*. New Haven: Yale University Press.

Alpers, Edward A. 2005. "'Mozambiques' in Brazil: Another Dimension of the African Diaspora in the New World." In José C. Curto and Renée Soulodre-La France, eds., *Africa and the Americas: Interconnections during the Slave Trade*. 1st ed. Trenton, N.J.: Africa World Press, 43–68.

Baralt, Guillermo A. 2007. *Slave Revolts in Puerto Rico*. Princeton: Markus Wiener.

Bastide, Roger, ed. 1975. *La Femme du Couleur en Amérique Latine*. Paris: Anthropos.

Bauer, Arnold J. 2001. *Goods, Power, History: Latin America's Material Culture*. Cambridge: Cambridge University Press.

Bauer, P. T. 1954. *West African Trade: A Study of Competition, Oligopoly and Monopoly in a Changing Economy*. Cambridge: Cambridge University Press.

Beck, Kurt, et al. 2004. *Blick nach vorn: Festgabe für Gerd Spittler zum 65. Geburtstag*. Cologne: Köppe.

Beckles, Hillary McD. 1991. "An Economic Life of Their Own: Slaves as Commodity Producers and Distributors in Barbados." In I. Berlin and Philip D. Morgan, eds., *The Slaves' Economy: Independent Production by Slaves in the Americas*. London: Frank Cass, 31–47.

———. 1998. "Capitalism, Slavery and Caribbean Modernity." *Callaloo* 20, 4: 777–789.

Bell, Madison Smartt. 2007. *Toussaint Louverture: A Biography*. New York: Pantheon Books.

Benedict, Ruth Fulton. 1948. "Anthropology and the Humanities." *American Anthropologist* 50,4: 585–593.

Benson, Lee. 1950. "Achille Loria's Influence on American Economic Thought." *Agricultural History* 24,3: 182–199.

Berger, Peter L. 1967. *The Sacred Canopy: Elements of a Sociological Theory of Religion*. Garden City, N.Y.: Doubleday.

Berlin, Ira, and Philip D. Morgan, eds. 1991. *The Slaves' Economy: Independent Production by Slaves in the Americas*. London, England; Portland, Ore: Frank Cass.

———. 1993. *Cultivation and Culture: Labor and the Shaping of Slave Life in the Americas*. Charlottesville: University Press of Virginia.

Besson, Jean. 2002. *Martha Brae's Two Histories: European Expansion and Caribbean Culture-building in Jamaica*. Chapel Hill: University of North Carolina Press.

Bohannan, Laura. 1966. "Shakespeare in the Bush." *Natural History* 75: 28–33.

Brathwaite, Kamau. 2005. *The Development of Creole Society in Jamaica, 1770–1820*. Oxford: Clarendon Press.

Brown, Vincent. 2008. *The Reaper's Garden: Death and Power in the World of Atlantic Slavery*. Cambridge, Mass.: Harvard University Press.

Burnard, Trevor. 2004. *Mastery, Tyranny and Desire: Thomas Thistlewood and His Slaves in the Anglo-Jamaican World*. Chapel Hill: University of North Carolina Press.

Carlyle, Thomas, John Stuart Mill, and Eugene R. August. 1971. *The Nigger Question: The Negro Question*. New York: Appleton-Century-Crofts.

Carnegie, Charles, ed., 1987. *Afro Caribbean Villages in Historical Perspective*. ACIJ Research Review, no. 2. Kingston: African Caribbean Institute of Jamaica.

Clark, Rev. John. 1852. *A Brief Account of the Settlements of the Emancipated Peasantry in the Neighbourhood of Brown's Town, Jamaica, in a Letter from John Clark, Missionary, to Joseph Sturge of Birmingham*. Birmingham, England.

Cohen, David William, and Jack P. Greene, eds. 1972. *Neither Slave nor Free: The Freedman of African Descent in the Slave Societies of the New World*. Baltimore: Johns Hopkins University Press.

Colthurst, John Bowen. 1977. *The Colthurst Journal: Journal of a Special Magistrate in the Islands of Barbados and St. Vincent, July 1835–August 1838*. Ed. Woodville K. Marshall. Millwood, N.Y.: KTO Press.

Comhaire, Jean. 1955. "The Haitian *Chef de Section*." *American Anthropologist* 57,4: 620–623.

Cooper, Frederick. 2005. *Colonialism in Question: Theory, Knowledge, History*. Berkeley: University of California Press.

Cooper, Frederick, Thomas C. Holt, and Rebecca J. Scott, eds. 2000. *Beyond Slavery: Explorations of Race, Labor, and Citizenship in Postemancipation Societies*. Chapel Hill: University of North Carolina Press.

Craton, Michael, and Garry Greenland. 1978. *Searching for the Invisible Man: Slaves and Plantation Life in Jamaica*. Cambridge, Mass.: Harvard University Press.

Craton, Michael, and James Walvin. 1970. *A Jamaican Plantation: The History of Worthy Park 1670–1970*. Toronto: University of Toronto Press.

Curto, José C., and Renée Soulodre-LaFrance, eds. 2005. *Africa and the Americas: Interconnections during the Slave Trade*. Trenton, N.J.: Africa World Press.

Davis, David Brion. 2003. *Challenging the Boundaries of Slavery*. Cambridge, Mass.: Harvard University Press.

Dayan, Joan. 1995. "Codes of Law and Bodies of Color." *New Literary History* 26,2: 283–308.

Deerr, Noel. 1949. *The History of Sugar*. Vol. 1. London: Chapman and Hall.

———. 1950. *The History of Sugar*. Vol. 2. London: Chapman and Hall.

De la Fuente, Alejandro. 2004. "Sugar and Slavery in Early Colonial Cuba." In Stuart B. Schwartz, ed., *Tropical Babylons: Sugar in the Making of the Atlantic World, 1450–1680*. Chapel Hill: University of North Carolina Press, 115–157.

Dubois, Laurent. 2004. *Avengers of the New World: The Story of the Haitian Revolution*. Cambridge, Mass.: Harvard University Press.

Dubois, Laurent, and John D. Garrigus. 2006. *Slave Revolution in the Caribbean, 1789–1804: A Brief History with Documents*. New York: Palgrave Macmillan.

Dubois, Laurent, and Julius Scott, eds. 2009. *Origins of the Black Atlantic*. Oxford: Routledge.

Du Bois, W. E. B. 1939. *Black Folk, Then and Now: An Essay in the History and Sociology of the Negro Race*. New York: Holt.

———. 1968. *The Autobiography of W. E. B. DuBois*. 1st ed. New York: International.

Du Bois, W. E. B., David W. Blight, and Robert Gooding-Williams. 1997. *The Souls of Black Folk*. Boston: Bedford Books. (Originally published 1903.)

Edwards, Bryan. 1793. *The History, Civil and Commercial, of the British Colonies in the West Indies*. London: Stockdale.

Elliott, John Huxtable. 2006. *Empires of the Atlantic World: Britain and Spain in America, 1492–1830*. New Haven: Yale University Press.

Eltis, David. 2000. *The Rise of African Slavery in the Americas*. Cambridge: Cambridge University Press.

Eltis, David, and David Richardson. 2008. *Extending the Frontiers: Essays on the New Transatlantic Slave Trade*. New Haven: Yale University Press.

Eriksen, Thomas Hylland. 2007. "Creolization in Anthropological Theory and in Mauritius." In Charles Stewart, ed., *Creolization: History. Ethnography. Theory*. Walnut Creek, Calif.: Left Coast Press, 153–177.

Fick, Carolyn. 1990. *The Making of Haiti: The Saint Domingue Revolution from Below*. Knoxville: University of Tennessee Press.

———. 1997. "The French Revolution in Saint Domingue: A Triumph or a Failure?" In David Barry Gaspar and David Patrick Geggus, eds. *A Turbulent Time: The*

French Revolution and the Greater Caribbean. Bloomington: University of Indiana Press. 51–77.

———— 2000. "Emancipation in Haiti: From Plantation Labor to Peasant Proprietorship." In Howard Temperley, ed., *After Slavery. Emancipation and Its Discontents*. London: Frank Cass, 11–401.

Figueroa, Luis A. 2005. *Sugar, Slavery, and Freedom in Nineteenth-century Puerto Rico*. Chapel Hill: University of North Carolina Press.

Firth, Raymond William, and Basil S. Yamey, eds. 1964. *Capital, Saving and Credit in Peasant Societies: Studies from Asia, Oceania, the Caribbean and Middle America*. Chicago: Aldine.

Friedmann, Harriet. 1999. "Circles of Growing and Eating: The Political Ecology of Food and Agriculture." In Raymond Grew, ed., *Food in Global History*. Boulder, Colo.: Westview Press, 33–57.

Friedmann, Harriet, and Philip McMichael. 1989. "Agriculture and the State System. The Rise and Decline of National Agricultures, 1870 to the Present." *Sociologia Ruralis*, 29,2: 93–117.

Funes Monzote, Reinaldo. 2008. *From Rainforest to Cane Field in Cuba: An Environmental History since 1492*. Chapel Hill: University of North Carolina Press.

Garrigus, John D. 2006. *Before Haiti: Race and Citizenship in French Saint-Domingue*. New York: Palgrave Macmillan.

Gaspar, David Barry, 1988. "Slavery, Amelioration, and Sunday Markets in Antigua, 1823–1831." *Slavery and Abolition* 9,1: 1–28.

————. 1992. "Working the System: Antigua Slaves and Their Struggle to Live." *Slavery and Abolition* 13,3: 131–135.

Gaspar, David Barry, and David Patrick Geggus, eds. 1997. *A Turbulent Time: The French Revolution and the Greater Carribean*. Bloomington: Indiana University Press.

Geggus, David. 1982. *Slavery, War, and Revolution: the British Occupation of Saint Domingue, 1793–1798*. Oxford: Oxford University Press.

————. 1983. *Slave Resistance Studies and the Saint Domingue Slave Revolt: Some Preliminary Considerations*. Miami: Florida International University.

————. 1997. "Slavery, War and Revolution in the Greater Caribbean, 1789–1815." In D. B. Gaspar and D. Geggus, eds., *A Turbulent Time. The French Revolution and the Greater Caribbean*. Bloomington: Indiana University Press, 1–50.

————. 2002. *Haitian Revolutionary Studies*. Bloomington: Indiana University Press.

Genovese, Eugene D. 1992. *From Rebellion to Revolution: Afro-American Slave Revolts in the Making of the Modern World*. Baton Rouge: Lousiana State University Press.

Geracimos, Ann. 2000. "Mystery in Miniature." *Smithsonian* 30,10: 20–21.

Giusti-Cordero, Juan. 1994. "Labor, Ecology and History in a Caribbean Sugar Plantation Region: Pinones (Loiza), Puerto Rico 1770–1950." Ph.D. diss., State University of New York, Binghamton.

———. 2009. "Beyond Sugar Revolutions. Rethinking the Spanish Caribbean in the Seventeenth and Eighteenth centuries." In G. Baca, A. Khan, and S. Palmié, eds., *Empirical Futures*. Chapel Hill: University of North Carolina Press, 58–83.

Grew, Raymond, ed. 1999. *Food in Global History*. Boulder, Colo.: Westview Press.

Hall, Catherine. 1992. *White, Male, and Middle-Class: Explorations in Feminism and History*. Cambridge: Polity Press.

———. 1993. "White Visions, Black Lives: The Free Villages of Jamaica." *History Workshop Journal* 36: 100–132.

Hall, Douglas. 1972. "Jamaica." In David W. Cohen and Jack P. Greene, eds., *Neither Slave nor Free*. Baltimore: Johns Hopkins University Press, 193–213.

Hannerz, Ulf. 1987. "The World in Creolization." *Africa* 57: 546–559.

———. 1992. *Cultural Complexity: Studies in the Social Organization of Meaning*. New York: Columbia University Press.

Herskovits, Melville J. 1930. "The Negro in the New World: The Statement of a Problem." *American Anthropologist* 32,1: 145–166.

Heuman, Gad J. 1981. *Between Black and White: Race, Politics, and the Free Coloreds in Jamaica, 1792–1865*. Westport, Conn.: Greenwood Press.

———. 1994. *"The Killing Time": The Morant Bay Rebellion in Jamaica*. London: Macmillan.

Higman, B. W. 1976. *Slave Population and Economy in Jamaica, 1807–1834*. Cambridge: Cambridge University Press.

Higman, B. W. 1984. *Slave Populations of the British Caribbean, 1807–1834*. Baltimore: Johns Hopkins University Press.

———. 1999. "The Internal Economy of Jamaican Pens, 1760–1890." In Verene A. Shepherd, ed., *Slavery without Sugar*. Gainesville: University of Florida Press, 63–81.

———. 2005. *Plantation Jamaica, 1750–1850: Capital and Control in a Colonial Economy*. Kingston, Jamaica: University of the West Indies Press.

Higman, B. W., George A. Aarons, Karlis Karklins, and Elizabeth Jean Reitz. 1998. *Montpelier, Jamaica: A Plantation Community in Slavery and Freedom, 1739–1912*. Mona, Jamaica: University of the West Indies Press.

Hochschild, Adam. 2005. *Bury the Chains: Prophets and Rebels in the Fight to Free an Empire's Slaves*. Boston: Houghton Mifflin.

Hoetink, H. 1967. *The Two Variants in Caribbean Race Relations: A Contribution to the Sociology of Segmented Societies.* London: Oxford University Press.

Hollander, Gail. 2008. *Raising Cane in the 'Glades: The Global Sugar Trade and the Transformation of Florida.* Chicago: University of Chicago Press.

Holt, Thomas C. 1982. "'An Empire over the Mind': Emancipation, Race and Ideology in the British West Indies and the South." In J. Morgan Kousser and James M. McPherson, eds., *Region, Race and Reconstruction.* New York: Oxford University Press, 283–314.

———. 1992. *The Problem of Freedom: Race, Labor, and Politics in Jamaica and Britain, 1832–1938.* Baltimore: Johns Hopkins University Press.

Hurwitz, Samuel J., and Edith F. Hurwitz. 1967. "A Token of Freedom: Private Bill Legislation for Free Negroes in Eighteenth-century Jamaica." *William and Mary Quarterly* 24,3: 423–431.

Hymes, Dell H., ed. 1964. *Language in Culture and Society: a Reader in Linguistics and Anthropology.* New York: Harper and Row.

———, ed. 1971. *Pidginization and Creolization of Languages: Proceedings of a Conference Held at the University of the West Indies, Mona, Jamaica, April, 1968.* Cambridge: Cambridge University Press.

James, C. L. R. 1963. *The Black Jacobins: Toussaint L'Ouverture and the San Domingo Revolution.* 2nd ed. New York: Vintage Books.

Johnson, Samuel. 1775. "Taxation No Tyranny: An Answer to the Resolutions and Address of the American Congress." London: Printed for T. Cadell.

Karttunen, Frances, and Alfred W. Crosby. 1995. "Language Death, Language Genesis, and World History." *Journal of World History* 6,2: 157–174.

Kiddy, Elizabeth W. 2005. "Kings, Queens, and Judges: Hierarchy in Lay Religious Brotherhoods of Blacks, 1750–1830." In José C. Curto and Renée Soulodre-La France, eds., *Africa and the Americas: Interconnections during the Slave Trade.* Trenton, N.J.: Africa World Press. 95–126.

Kinsbruner, Jay. 1996. *Not of Pure Blood: The Free People of Color and Racial Prejudice in Nineteenth-Century Puerto Rico.* Durham, N.C.: Duke University Press.

Knox, A. J. G. 1977. "Opportunities and Opposition: The Rise of Jamaica's Black Peasantry and the Nature of Planter Resistance." *Canadian Review of Sociology and Anthropology* 14,4: 381–395.

Konetzke, Richard. 1946. *El Imperio Español.* Madrid: Nueva Época.

Kousser, J. Morgan, and James M. McPherson, eds. 1982. *Region, Race and Reconstruction.* New York: Oxford University Press.

Kriger, Colleen E. 2005. "The Conundrum of Culture in Atlantic History." In José C. Curto and Renée Soulodre-La France, eds., *Africa and the Americas: Interconnections during the Slave Trade.* Trenton, N.J.: Africa World Press, 259–278.

Kroeber, A. L. 1948. *Anthropology: Race, Language, Culture, Psychology, Pre-History.* New York: Harcourt, Brace.

Kukla, Jon. 2003. *A Wilderness so Immense: the Louisiana Purchase and the Destiny of America.* New York: A. A. Knopf.

Lahav, Pnina. 1975. "The Chef de Section: Structure and Functions of Haiti's Basic Administrative Institution." In Sidney W. Mintz, ed., *Working Papers in Haitian Society and Culture.* New Haven: Antilles Research Program, Yale University, 51–81.

Lewis, David Levering. 1993. *W. E. B. Du Bois—Biography of a Race, 1868–1919.* New York: Holt.

Leyburn, James Graham. 1966. *The Haitian People.* New Haven: Yale University Press.

Lichtenstein, Alex. 1988. "'That Disposition to Theft with Which They Have Been Branded': Moral Economy, Slave Management and the Law." *Journal of Social History* 21,3: 413–40.

———. 1998. "Was the Emancipated Slave a Proletarian?" *Reviews in American History* 26,1: 124–145.

Marx, Karl, and Friedrich Engels. 1967. *Capital: A Critique of Political Economy.* New York: International.

Mathieson, William Law. 1926. *British Slavery and Its Abolition, 1823–1838.* London: Longmans, Green.

Matory, James Lorand. 2005. *Black Atlantic Religion: Tradition, Transnationalism, and Matriarchy in the Afro-Brazilian Candomblé.* Princeton: Princeton University Press.

McClellan, James E. 1992. *Colonialism and Science: Saint Domingue in the Old Regime.* Baltimore: Johns Hopkins University Press.

McConnell, H. Ormonde. 1957. *You Can Learn Creole.* Petit-Goâve, Haiti: Imprimerie du Sauveur.

McNeill, John Robert, and William Hardy McNeill. 2003. *The Human Web: A Bird's-eye View of World History.* New York: Norton.

Merivale, Herman. 1967. *Lectures on Colonization and Colonies.* New York: Kelley.

Merrill, William L., and Ives Goddard, eds. 2002. *Anthropology, History, and American Indians: Essays in Honor of William Curtis Sturtevant.* Washington, D.C.: Smithsonian Institution Press.

Métraux, Alfred. 1951. *Making a Living in the Marbial Valley.* Occasional Papers in Education no. 10. Paris: UNESCO.

Mintz, Sidney W. 1951. "The Role of Forced Labour in Nineteenth Century Puerto Rico." *Caribbean Historical Review* 2: 131–141.

———. 1955. "The Jamaican Internal Marketing Pattern: Some Notes and Hypotheses." *Social and Economic Studies* 4,1: 95–103.

———. 1956. "Cañamelar: The Subculture of a Rural Sugar Plantation Proletariat."

In Julian H. Steward et al., eds., *The People of Puerto Rico*. Urbana: University of Illinois Press, 314–417.

———. 1957. "The Role of the Middleman in the Internal Distribution System of a Caribbean Peasant Economy." *Human Organization* 15,2: 18–23.

———. 1958a. "Historical Sociology of the Jamaican Church-Founded Free Village system." *De West-Indische Gids* 38,1: 46–70.

———. 1958b. "Labor and Sugar in Puerto Rico and Jamaica." *Comparative Studies in Society and History* 1,3: 273–283.

———. 1960a. "A Tentative Typology of Eight Haitian Market Places." *Revista de Ciencias Sociales* 4,1: 15–58.

———. 1960b. *Worker in the Cane*. New Haven: Yale University Press.

———. 1961. "The Question of Caribbean Peasantries: A Comment." *Caribbean Studies* 1,3: 31–34.

———. 1964. "The Employment of Capital by Haitian Market Women." In Raymond Firth and Basil Yamey, eds., *Capital, Savings and Credit in Peasant Societies*. Chicago: Aldine, 256–286.

———. 1966. "The Caribbean as a Sociocultural Area." *Cahiers d'histoire mondiale* 10,4: 912–937.

———. 1967. "Caribbean Nationhood in Anthropological Perspective." In S. Lewis and T. Mathews, eds., *Caribbean Integration*. Río Piedras: Institute of Caribbean Studies, 141–154.

———. 1971a. "The Socio-historical Background of Pidginization and Creolization." In Dell Hymes, ed., *Pidginization and Creolization of Languages*. Cambridge: Cambridge University Press, 153–168.

———. 1971b. "Toward an Afro-American History." *Cahiers d'histoire mondiale* 13,2: 317–332.

———. 1973. "A Note on the Definition of the Peasantry." *Journal of Peasant Studies* 1,3: 91–106.

———. 1974. *Caribbean Transformations*. Chicago: Aldine.

———. 1975. "Les rôles économiques et la tradition culturelle." In Roger Bastide, ed., *La femme du couleur en Amérique Latine*. Paris: Anthropos, 115–148.

———. 1977. "North American Anthropological Contributions to Caribbean Studies." *Boletín de Estudios Latinoamericanos y del Caribe*: 60–82.

———. 1978. "Caribbean Marketplaces and Caribbean History." *Nova Americana* 8,1: 5–16.

———. 1979. "Slavery and the Rise of Peasantry." *Historical Reflections* 6,1: 215–242.

———. 1984. *From Plantations to Peasantries in the Caribbean*. Washington, D.C.: Woodrow Wilson International Center Latin American Program.

————. 1985. *Sweetness and Power*. New York: Viking-Penguin.

————. 1989. "The Sensation of Moving, While Standing Still." *American Ethnologist* 16,4: 786–796.

————. 1993. *Goodbye Columbus: Second Thoughts on the Caribbean Region at Mid-Millennium*. The 1993 Walter Rodney Memorial Lecture. Coventry: University of Warwick.

————. 1995. "Can Haiti Change?" *Foreign Affairs* 74,1: 73–86.

————. 1996. "Enduring Substances, Trying Theories: The Caribbean Region as Ec-umene." *Journal of the Royal Anthropological Institute* 2,2: 289–311.

————. 1997. "The Localization of Anthropological Practice: From Area Studies to Transnationalism." *Critique of Anthropology* 18,2: 117–133.

————. 2002. "Quenching Homologous Thirsts." In William L. Merrill and Ives Goddard, eds., *Anthropology, History, and American Indians: Essays in Honor of William Curtis Sturtevant*. Smithsonian Contributions to Anthropology no. 44. Washington, D.C.: Smithsonian Institution Press, 349–357.

————. 2004. "Caribbean History, Caribbean Labor." In Kurt Beck, Till Förster, and Hans Peter Hahn, eds., *Blick nach vorn; Festgabe für Gerd Spittler zum 65. Geburtstag*. Cologne: Rüdiger Köppe, 136–144.

Mintz, Sidney W., and Harriet Friedmann. 2004. "Colonialismo e Prima Mondializ-zazione." In Massimo Montanari and Françoise Sabban, eds., *Atlante Dell'Alimen-tazione e Della Gastronomia*. Turin: UTET, 358–371.

Mintz, Sidney W., and Douglas Hall. 1960. "The Origins of the Jamaican Internal Marketing System." In *Papers in Caribbean Anthropology, Yale University Publica-tions in Anthropology* 57. New Haven, 3–26.

Mintz, Sidney W. and Richard Price. 1976. *The Birth of African-American Culture*. Boston: Beacon Press.

Mintz, Sidney W., and Eric R. Wolf. 1950. "An Analysis of Ritual Co-parenthood (Compadrazgo)." *Southwestern Journal of Anthropology* 6,4: 341–368.

Mitchell, Joseph. 1943. *McSorley's Wonderful Saloon*. New York: Duell, Sloan and Pearce.

Moral, Paul. 1978. *Le paysan haïtien: Étude sur la vie rurale en Haïti*. Port-au-Prince: Éditions Fardin.

Moreau de St. Méry, Louis. 1797. *Description topographique, physique, civile, politique et historique de la partie française de l'isle Saint Domingue*, 3 vols. Paris: Société de l'Histoire des Colonies Françaises et Librairie LaRose (1958)

Moreno Fraginals, Manuel, and Luis M. Traviesas. 1978. *El ingenio: Complejo económico social cubano del azúcar*. Havana: Editorial de Ciencias Sociales, 1978.

Morgan, Philip D. 1998. *Slave Counterpoint: Black Culture in the Eighteenth-century Chesapeake and Lowcountry*. Chapel Hill: University of North Carolina Press.

Napoléon. 1858–70. *Correspondance de Napoléon 1er*. Paris: H. Plon, J. Dumaine.

Nishida, Mieko. 2003. *Slavery and Identity: Ethnicity, Gender, and Race in Salvador, Brazil, 1808–1888*. Bloomington: Indiana University Press.

Palmie, Stephan. 2007a. "The 'C' Word Again: From Colonial to Postcolonial Semantics." In Charles Stewart, ed. *Creolization: History. Ethnography. Theory*. Walnut Creek, Calif.: Left Coast Press, 66–83.

———. 2007b. "Is There a Model in the Muddle? Creolization in African Americanist History and Anthropology." In Charles Stewart, ed., *Creolization: History. Ethnography. Theory*. Walnut Creek, Calif.: Left Coast Press, 178–200.

Parés, Luis Nicolau. 2005. "Tranformations of the Sea and Thunder Voduns in the Gbe-Speaking Area and in the Bahian Jeje Candomblé." In José C. Curto and Renée Souloudre-La France, eds., *Africa and the Americas: Interconnections during the Slave Trade*. Trenton, N.J.: Africa World Press, 69–94.

Paton, Diana. 2004. *No Bond but the Law: Punishment, Race, and Gender in Jamaican State Formation, 1780–1870*. Durham, N.C.: Duke University Press.

Patterson, Orlando. 1967a. *An Absence of Ruins*. London: Hutchinson.

———. 1967b. *The Sociology of Slavery: An Analysis of the Origins, Development and Structure of Negro Slave Society in Jamaica*. London: MacGibbon and Kee.

———. 1982. *Slavery and Social Death: A Comparative Study*. Cambridge, Mass.: Harvard University Press.

Picó, Fernando. 2006. *History of Puerto Rico: A Panorama of Its People*. English ed. Princeton: Markus Wiener.

Price, Richard. 1966. "Caribbean Fishing and Fishermen: A Historical Sketch." *American Anthropologist* 68,4: 1363–1383.

Ramos Mattei, Andrés. 1985. "Technical Innovations and Social Change in the Sugar Industry of Puerto Rico, 1870–1880." In M. Moreno Fraginals, F. Moya Pons, and S. L. Engerman, eds., *Between Slavery and Free Labor: the Spanish-speaking Caribbean in the Nineteenth Century*. Baltimore: Johns Hopkins University Press.

———. 1988. *La sociedad del azúcar en Puerto Rico, 1870–1910*. Río Piedras: Universidad de Puerto Rico.

Rediker, Marcus. 2007. *The Slave Ship*. New York: Viking.

Reinecke, John. 1964. "Trade Jargons and Creole Dialects as Marginal Languages." In Dell Hymes, ed., *Language in Culture and Society*. New York: Harper and Row, 534–546.

Rodriguez Morel, Genaro. 2004. "The Sugar Economy of Española in the Sixteenth Century." In Stuart B. Schwartz, ed., *Tropical Babylons: Sugar and the Making of the Atlantic World, 1450–1680*. Chapel Hill: University of North Carolina Press, 85–114.

Rogozinski, Jan. 2000. *A Brief History of the Caribbean: From the Arawak and Carib to the Present.* New York: Plume.

Roumain, Jacques. 1944. *À propos de la campagne anti-superstitieuse.* Port-au-Prince: Imprimerie de l'État.

Scarano, Francisco A. 1984. *Sugar and Slavery in Puerto Rico: The Plantation Economy of Ponce, 1800–1850.* Madison: University of Wisconsin Press.

———. 1989. "Congregate and Control: The Peasantry and Labor Coercion in Puerto Rico before the Age of Sugar: 1750–1820." *New West Indian Guide* 63,1: 23–40.

Schultze, Ernst. 1933. "Sklaven- und Dienersprachen (Sogen. Handelssprachen)." *Sociologus* 9: 377–418.

Schwartz, Stuart B., ed. 2004. *Tropical Babylons: Sugar and the Making of the Atlantic World, 1450–1680.* Chapel Hill: University of North Carolina Press.

Scott, David. 2004. "Modernity That Predated the Modern: Sidney Mintz's Caribbean." *History Workshop Journal* 58,1: 191–210.

Scott, Julius Sherrard. 1986. "The Common Wind: Currents of Afro-American Communication in the Era of the Haitian Revolution." Ph. D. diss., Duke University.

Scott, Rebecca J. 1985. *Slave Emancipation in Cuba: The Transition to Free Labor, 1860–1899.* Princeton: Princeton University Press.

———. 2001. "Reclaiming Gregoria's Mule: The Meaning of Freedom in the Arimao and Caunao Valleys, Cienfuegos, Cuba, 1880–1889." *Past and Present* 170: 181–216.

———. 2005. *Degrees of Freedom: Louisiana and Cuba after Slavery.* Cambridge, Mass.: Harvard University Press.

Service, Elman R. 1955. "Indo-European Relations in Colonial Latin America." *American Anthropologist* 57,3: 411–425.

Sewell, William Grant. 1968. *The Ordeal of Free Labor in the British West Indies.* London: Cass.

Sheller, Mimi. 2000. *Democracy after Slavery: Black Publics and Peasant Radicalism in Haiti and Jamaica.* Gainesville: University Press of Florida.

Shepherd, Verene, ed. 2002. *Slavery without Sugar: Diversity in Caribbean Economy and Society since the Seventeenth Century.* Gainesville: University Press of Florida.

Shepherd, Verene A., and Kathleen E. A. Monteith. 2002. "Pen-keepers and Coffee Farmers in a Sugar-plantation Economy." In Verene A. Shepherd, ed., *Slavery without Sugar: Diversity in Caribbean Economy and Society since the Seventeenth Century.* Gainesville: University Press of Florida, 82–101.

Sheridan, Richard B. 1973. *Sugar and Slavery: An Economic History of the British West Indies, 1623–1775.* Baltimore: Johns Hopkins University Press.

Shilliam, Robert. 2008. "What the Haitian Revolution Might Tell Us about Development, Security and the Politics of Race." *Comparative Studies in Society and History* 50,3: 778–808.

Skaggs, Jimmy M. 1994. *The Great Guano Rush: Entrepreneurs and American Overseas Expansion.* New York: St. Martin's Press.

Smith, S. D. 2002. "Coffee and the 'Poorer Sort of People' in Jamaica during the Period of African Enslavement." In Verene A. Shepherd, ed., *Slavery without Sugar.* Gainesville: University Press of Florida, 102–128.

Steward, Julian Haynes, Robert A. Manners, Eric R. Wolf, Elena Padilla Seda, Sidney W. Mintz, and Raymond L. Scheele, eds. 1956. *The People of Puerto Rico: A Study in Social Anthropology.* Urbana: University of Illinois Press.

Stewart, Charles. 2007. *Creolization: History, Ethnography, Theory.* Walnut Creek, Calif.: Left Coast Press.

Tambiah, Stanley Jeyaraja. 1985. *Culture, Thought, and Social Action: An Anthropological Perspective.* Cambridge, Mass.: Harvard University Press.

Thompson, Edgar Tristram. 1932. "The Plantation." Ph.D. diss., University of Chicago.

Trouillot, Michel-Rolph. 1982. "Motion in the System: Coffee, Color and Slavery in Eighteenth-century Saint-Domingue." *Review (Fernand Braudel Center)* 50,3: 331–388.

———. 1995. *Silencing the Past: Power and the Production of History.* Boston: Beacon Press.

Turits, Richard Lee. 2003. *Foundations of Despotism: Peasants, the Trujillo Regime, and Modernity in Dominican History.* Stanford: Stanford University Press.

Turnbull, David. 1840. *Travels in the West: Cuba; with Notices of Porto Rico and the Slave Trade.* London: Longman, Orme, Brown, Green, and Longmans.

U.S. Department of Commerce, Bureau of Foreign and Domestic Commerce. 1917. *The Cane Sugar Industry.* Miscellaneous Series No. 53. Washington: Government Printing Office.

Wallerstein, Immanuel M. 2004. *World-Systems Analysis: An Introduction.* Durham, N.C.: Duke University Press.

Warner-Lewis, Maureen. 2003. *Central Africa in the Caribbean.* Kingston, Jamaica: University of the West Indies Press.

Watts, David. 1987. *The West Indies: Patterns of Development, Culture, and Environmental Change since 1492.* Cambridge: Cambridge University Press.

Weisskoff, Richard. 1985. *Factories and Food Stamps: The Puerto Rico Model of Development.* Baltimore: Johns Hopkins University Press.

Williams, Eric Eustace. 1944. *Capitalism and Slavery.* Chapel Hill: University of North Carolina Press.

Williams, James. 2001. *A Narrative of Events since the First of August, 1834, by James Williams, an Apprenticed Labourer in Jamaica*. Ed. Diana Paton. Durham, N.C.: Duke University Press.

Wolf, Eric R. 1956. "San Jose: Subcultures of a "Traditional" Coffee Muncipality." In Julian H. Steward et al., eds., *The People of Puerto Rico: A Study in Social Anthropology*. Urbana: University of Illinois Press, 171–264.

———. 1966. *Peasants*. Englewood Cliffs, N.J.: Prentice-Hall.

———. 1982. *Europe and the People without History*. Berkeley: University of California Press.

Wright, Irene. 1916. *The Early History of Cuba, 1492–1586*. New York: Macmillan.

Zenón Cruz, Isabelo. 1975. *Narciso descubre su trasero: El negro en la cultura puerterriqueña*. Humacao, Puerto Rico: Editorial Furidi.

Zeuske, Michael. 2006. *Sklaven und Sklaverei in den Welten des Atlantiks, 1400–1490*. Berlin: LIT.

Index

Abolition, 4, 9; role of churches in, 60–61; freedom vs., 27; in Haiti, 90, 91, 92; in Jamaica, 45, 56–61; in Puerto Rico, 145–146, 146–147

Adrien, Anaïs (Nana), 123–131, 132

Africa: colonialism in, 6; cultural continuity and, 202–204; Du Bois on, 4–5; markets in, 131; sources of slaves in, 196–197

Afro-America, 45–46

Agriculture. *See* Farms; Plantations

American Revolution, 93–95, 97–98

Angwin Crawl, Jamaica, 65

Anthropology: aims of, 21–22; cultural theory in, 198, 205; on culture change/acculturation, 201; Du Bois and, 1–5; on folk categories, 176; history and, 14, 22–23; on primitive vs. westernized societies, 42–43; training in, 18

Antilles: in Caribbean metaregion, 44–45; colonialism in, 6; Du Bois on, 4; Greater, 25; labor in, 184; Lesser, 25

Apprenticeship: in Jamaica, 27, 56, 63; in Puerto Rico, 27, 30

Architecture, 184

Bahamas, 25

Bananas, 114–115

Barbados: colonization of, 5; English control of, 47, 48; farming in, 33

Beckford, William, 184

Bee, Rev. John, 67

Belnavis, Catherine, 66, 67

Belnavis, Leah, 66, 67, 81, 82

Belnavis, Thelma, 66, 67

Belnavis, Tom, 66, 67–69, 76, 81, 82, 132; access to cash by, 161; meaning of land to, 82–84; on race, 86

Berger, Peter L., 200

Besson, Jean, 83

Black Atlantic, 45–46

Black Folk, Then and Now (Du Bois), 4–5

Black Jacobins, The (James), 11–12

Blagrove, Peter, 80

Blanco, Tomás, 135

Boas, Franz, 4

Bossal, 188

Boyer, Jean Pierre, 95, 112

Bozal, 188

Brathwaite, Kamau, 16, 107

Brazil, 92: slavery in, 4, 186; sugar production in, 47

Brown, Vincent, 13–14